TRAPPED IN THE (
"The story behind the documentary Voice of Blood"

Tony Angastiniotis

RUSTEM BOOKSHOP

Trapped in the Green Line
The story behind the documentary Voice of Blood

First Edition.

ISBN 975-98959-9-4

Design:
Rustem Bookshop

Cover Graphics:
Beren Doğan

Cover Photograph:
İsa Sağlam

English Translation:
Robin Davie

Editing:
Aslı Giray

RUSTEM
Kyrenia Street 22/24
PO Box: 239, Nicosia – North Cyprus
Tel: (0392)228 35 06 - (0392) 227 24 55
Web Page: http:/www.rustemkitabevi.com
            http:/www.rustembookshop.com
e-mail: rustemkitabevi@superonline.com

CONTENTS

To die for one's country
is the duty of each citizen.
However, nobody has to lie for its sake.

Charles de Montesquieu

I would like to thank everyone who accompanied me in my lonely sky, and who left their traces in my heart.

I understand the ones who are so passionately against my work. I will probably never understand the silence of my friends, but anyway, this work is not for them.

It is for my children Andria, Dimitris, Lois and Nefeli, who put their trust in me expecting that I will provide a better tomorrow for them.

AUTHOR'S NOTE

When I began to write this book, in order to promote my documentary mainly to the Greek Cypriots who would not probably have a chance to watch it on the Greek channels, I never thought that anybody from outside Cyprus would become interested in my work. A few months after the release of my first interviews in local newspapers, many emails came from around the world, as far as Brazil, asking for my documentary. I guess I didn't take into consideration the power of internet and the hundreds of Cypriots that are scattered around the world who follow the local news through the net. Through the year, many journalists and documentarists from different countries flew in to the island just to interview me. Although it was Turkish and Turkish Cypriot media that was mostly interviewing me, it was an article from a Greek (English language) newspaper that made the difference.

Just when I started losing hope that my documentary and my peace efforts would never reach beyond North Cyprus, a phone call changed my destiny. In a very small coffee shop in Voulgaroktonou Street, located in the old city of Nicosia, a journalist from Cyprus Mail, Simon Bahceli gave me a platform. His article with the title **'Frozen out': Greek Cypriot battles to have documentary on 1974 killings aired"** was later found in many news web pages from *Le Figaro* to Official European Union pages, to chat rooms.

Due to the fact that many of the Cypriots have had the chance to understand my views and beliefs by following my interviews in newspapers and TV programs, something harder for the foreigners, I decided to insert two chapters in the beginning of the English version to help the readers understand better the environment in which the book was written. Chapter three of the book is really the foreword of the Greek and Turkish versions, and chapter 13 their conclusion. For the same reason I have added the chapters in the beginning, I have also added the newspaper articles after the conclusion.

If sometime in the later chapters some arguments seem to be a repetitive, this is due to the fact that I didn't want to disturb my line of thought when writing the two new chapters, and for this you must forgive me.

Tony Angastiniotis
August 2005

CHAPTER 1
BEYOND PROPAGANDA

"Get the facts, or the facts will get you. And when you get them, get them right, or they will get you wrong."
Thomas Fuller

I was born in Aberdeen Scotland in 1966 and moved to Cyprus in 1970. My father, a Greek Cypriot doctor, whose family roots are located in the small village of Angastina (Aslankoy), on the main road between Famagusta and Nicosia, was born and raised in the city of Famagusta. On our return to Cyprus my father was appointed as a pediatrician in the Famagusta General Hospital, so Famagusta became the place of my first childhood memories until the 1974 war.

Throughout the war days my mother was in Scotland with my younger brother and my father was on duty in the hospital, so my two sisters and I were taken care of by our grandparents. We fled the city with a taxi, taking with us only a suitcase with our necessary clothing, thinking we would return back in a few days. My father stayed behind and as he told us later, he and a nurse were of the last to abandon the city after realizing that no more wounded were coming in and the Greek army had deserted the city, allowing the Turkish army to capture it without a shot fired. I will never forget my father's words when describing the incident: "As we drove off towards Derinia, we stopped the car and from a hill we gazed at the city and shed bitter tears. I decided not to cut off my moustache until the day I returned back home." He kept his vow!

On the 23rd of April 2003, the barricades that for 29 years kept us separated from our beloved hometown were opened and even as visitors we would be able to see our home city again. Most of the city is locked behind military fence, and so was my grandparents' house. The house we were renting, where all my childhood memories laid, was just outside the fenced area.

We waited 12 long hours on a mile-long queue to pass with our car from the Ledra Palace checkpoint, and we were willing to wait 12 more if necessary. You could never trust in those days that the barricades would stay open for ever. As I drove with my wife through the Mesaoria plain towards Famagusta, a sorrowful "why!" was slipping recursively from our lips. Why on earth did all this happen, why the division, why three long decades?

As I arrived in the city, although I was 8 years old when I left, I knew exactly how to drive straight to my home. I guess when we left that hot summer of 1974 our souls stayed behind waiting for our return. As we parked outside the front door of what was once my home, I was not able to withhold my tears. To this day I don't remember ever weeping so overwhelmingly. Nothing had changed; even the Egyptian plum trees were still there. Two old women opened the door and realizing who we were, they welcomed us in. On the corridor wall in front of us, my father's graduation picture and his medical diploma were still hanging on the wall waiting to be collected. "Why have you kept it there?" I asked the old woman. "We are from Paphos" she said, "we never felt that this home belonged to us" and she went on to apologize for not painting the ceiling.

I was shocked! It was not only us who hoped that one day we would return back to our homes, but also this Turkish Cypriot woman, thus she kept the pictures and diploma on the wall and worried that I would   find my ceiling in a bad condition. "What kind of an enemy is this?" I thought, "What manner of hatred is this? What about that entire "barbarian" preachy I was taught?"

In fact nothing in the North was as we expected. For years the Greek propaganda was leading us to believe that the Turkish Cypriots were living in very poor conditions and were waiting for us to save them from poverty and depression. I wondered what on earth they had been hearing about our standard of living. I had crossed the borders a few times in the past as a cameraman, but only to walk a few meters to Denktaş' office for news coverage, and though I didn't see much, I knew that it wasn't as bad as we had been told, but for my wife it was a shock. As we drove through Nicosia center to reach the main road to Famagusta, she was astonished when she saw a four- lane road (outside the Turkish embassy), and even more astonished when some Mercedes and other luxury cars passed by. "They have roads, they have good cars and they have houses," she screamed. "Yes, and they don't have horns on their heads and tails" I replied. "When I was a child," she continued, "I don't know why, but I imagined the Turks as giants that ate tins and somehow this concept resided with me".

Those first few months we had crossed the borders a few more times with my wife, just to travel around the island and visit some of the beauties our eyes were deprived of for so many years. It was on these long journeys that we truly started to have close encounters with Turkish Cypriot compatriots. Soon we discovered they were humans, they did not have horns and tails and definitely were not eating tins. Actually in general, they were very hospitable people, good hearted, always welcoming us with an enormous smile that made it impossible for us to reject their invitations for a cup of coffee, or even sometimes a whole meal. "So where on earth are the barbarians?" we thought time and time again.

It soon became obvious that most things we have heard about these people was not even close to the truth. We began to think about the sources we were getting all this information through the years of separation, schools, family, media and politicians. Were they all lying? Were they all part of a great conspiracy? Did they repeat the lies so many times that they even believed they were true? Our generation had never mixed with the Turkish Cypriots so all that we had been receiving was secondhand information. All we heard over and over again were the elderly calling them dogs.

Though I am not a Buddhist, there is something Buddha said worth noticing: *"Do not believe in anything simply because you have heard it. Do not believe in anything simply because it is spoken and rumoured by many. Do not believe in anything simply because it is found written in your religious books. Do not believe in anything merely on the authority of your teachers and elders. Do not believe in traditions because they have been handed down for many generations. But after observation and analysis, when you find that anything agrees with reason and is conducive to the good and benefit of one and all, then accept it and live up to it."*

Turks are the Greeks' ultimate enemy and that is the end of the story. Even our Orthodox religion gave us permission to hate them. My wife's aunty, a very religious elderly woman who has never been to school, was trying to convince me one day that the Turks stink because they are not baptized. How did she develop this belief? "Ask the priest" she said. I heard the village priest in the coffee shop calling the Turks dogs. I patted him on the shoulder and asked him if he believed the Bible. This priest, as many of his colleagues, has enough religion to manufacture hate, but not enough to create love, but what can you expect from a religion that forces you into membership by child baptism without asking you. Not even your parents respect you enough to give you a chance to choose a religion. You are Greek and you are Orthodox and that's the end of the story. Nationalism is higher even from Jesus' essential teaching, *"Love your enemies, bless them that curse you, do good to them that hate you, and pray for them which despitefully use you, and persecute you."* (Matthew 5: 44)

It's been clear to me that the fundamental nationalism is a basic element within the Greek community not limited to the right or the left wing parties, but you cannot simply blame the people. It is something that is so strongly imposed on them from a very young age that it becomes part of their culture. This is the reason most people are not able to acknowledge the presence of extreme nationalism; it's been their nourishment from their nappy days, grafted in the veins on the first vaccination.

Many will argue that I am drawing the longbow. It's important to understand that this is not a conclusion I have made after reading a book; this is not borrowed information, this is many years of first hand experience, but beyond my experience there are enough facts that cannot be ignored. A Jawaharlal Nehru said some time ago, *"Facts are facts and will not disappear on account of your likes"*.

But what are the recent facts?

The pre-referendum period was probably the most aggressive period I can remember ever since 1974. With the majority rejecting the Annan Plan (75%), the Yes voters were attacked psychologically and in many occasions physically. The island was divided into "pro-No" and "pro-Yes". Cars that had a "Yes" sign on them were smashed, and with no hesitation some politicians and journalists were calling the "Yes" supporters traitors who got money from the CIA. Everywhere you turned, your eyes you could see the word "No". It was hanging from building tops to electric poles. "Yes" banners were forcefully removed, and in one incident a woman who tried to replace a small banner, that was removed moments after she placed it on a pole, were arrested. The situation was out of control. Long life friendships and even family relationships were influenced by the fanaticism that arose. At my working place I was asked in a mocking way if I had Turkish windows on my computer, but I was luckier than others (not in my company) who lost their jobs.

The Media was also dancing to the same rhythm. Ex-EOKA B member, Mr. Koutsou and his party leaders, whose party has no more than 3%, had more time on talk shows than the pro-Yes DISY party leaders, that is the biggest party on the island with 34%. CYBC, the national TV station refused to give time to European official Mr. Verhoegen, and friends working in the station have said to me that a list with pro-Yes employees was made by the station board, and their jobs were threatened. DISY leader, Mr. Anastasiades, made a protest to the European Council about CYBC's unequal handling of all opinions. A grenade was thrown on his bedroom veranda, and a death threat followed for him and his family if he didn't withdraw his complaints. Nobody was arrested, and a few days later, the complaints were withdrawn. I was in a bookshop in Nicosia that morning where a sweet young saleswoman said in a loud voice to her colleague, "I am glad they bombed the traitor," and the people around her smiled in conformity.

The church likewise used its influence and bishops were declaring that anybody voting "Yes" would go to hell. They even went as far as to promise the refugees that were to return under the Annan plan that they would give them compensations for their 1974 home losses. A promise they never fulfilled of course.

After President Papadopoulos returned to Cyprus, it was promised that the basic chapters of the Annan plan would be printed by the government and be sent to all households. I am still waiting for mine, so are my neighbors and all others whom I have asked.

Ignorance has always been a good way to handle the masses. Knowledge is power! So let's keep the people ignorant and control their minds and behaviors. But what happens if somebody breaks through the propaganda wall, like Tony did, and exposes some truth to the people that hasn't been exposed before and is opposite to the government line. Don't worry we will label him a traitor and some hot-blooded patriot will remove him from the earth, and the people will say "amen, he got what he deserved."

I think Mark Twain saw the future politicians when he wrote more than a century ago, *"Get your facts first, and then you can distort them as much as you please"*. If all these facts don't prove anything of what I claim, I must be a very disturbed person with a castle in the sky. Who knows, maybe I am?

I know that through my text many will forerun to judge me as anti-Greek. If I were anti-Greek it would mean I am anti-Tony, because I am also part of the Greek community. My intentions are not to accuse but look the community structure in the eyes and through honest analysis find the errors and deal with them. You can never change the counterfeit, only the authentic is alterable. We cannot change who we think we are; we can only change who we really are. The problem was not that the Greek community decided to reject the Annan plan. We can have hundreds of plans coming our way through the years that the Turkish Cypriots may reject and the Greek Cypriots accept. It is the how we rejected, the aggressiveness that was manifested throughout that

8

proves my point. I could go through historical incidents to prove my point but the issue is not the past but the fact that the demons are still around.

Somebody may ask, what is wrong with loving your nation and supporting your community? Nothing, if you don't become aggressive even with your family members, smash cars, sack your employees, rejoice when a politician you disagree with is bombed, label those who disagree with you as traitors paid from CIA, threaten old ladies with eternal damnation. Is not all this deficiency of democracy? And is it not abnormality when the crowd justifies this aggressiveness as national obligation? And doesn't this attitude create a credibility gap from the minority that is attacked just because of their disagreement? Some will claim that they didn't get involved in such confrontations. Isn't the silence witness to a crime equally guilty as the criminal? Wasn't the lady in the bookshop as guilty as the one throwing the grenade?

CHAPTER 2
IF I PERISH, I PERISH

"The ultimate measure of a man is not where he stands in moments of comfort, but where he stands at times of challenge and controversy."

Martin Luther King, Jr.

Are you a pro-Turk Tony? I am glad you asked. This is one of the problems of our time. Many Turkish Cypriots are pro-Greek, and many Greek Cypriots are pro- Turkish.

The pro-Greeks are mainly anti-Denktaş campaigners and Annan plan supporters that refuse to come in terms with some of the realities about the Greeks mentioned in the previous chapter. They argued that it was Denktaş' Taksim policy that kept the two communities separated; thinking that if they got rid of Denktaş the communities would again unite. They got a slap in the face on the 24th of April 2004 after the referendum and some still refuse to see the reality; according to my view, the problem was not just Denktaş' inflexible approach.

The pro-Turks are the Greeks that passionately supported the Annan plan. These are people who believed that the Annan plan was the best and last chance for the two communities to reunite and if not this would lead to the final separation. These people saw in Papadopoulos, the Greek president, another hardliner Denktaş arising, thus gave him the nick name

10

Denktasopoulos. They believed that the Turkish Cypriots had also suffered in the hands of the Greeks back in the sixties but they were willing to apologize and move on into a new beginning. They also got a slap in the face during the referendum. Realizing that Papadopoulos was not the only one to be blamed, 75% of the Greek community had the same mentality as him, even many left wingers.

I am pro-Cypriot. I believe that this island belongs to both its people. I would not support any policy I view as wrong from whatever side it is coming. I see both nationalities as my compatriots, equal in status. Before 1974 the Greek leadership had the upper hand and abused their authority against the Turks in an effort to achieve Enosis, unity with Greece. In 1974, the Turkish leadership got the upper hand through the Turkish intervention, and kept the status quo long enough for separation to be established. To say the people are victimized by the politicians can never be accepted because politicians are voted by the people; hence the majority was in agreement with them. Of course the fact that people were often misled by the leaderships, and the leaderships many times misestimated situations cannot be ignored.

Pro-Cypriot means there is no other side. Making a one-sided documentary and be called a traitor was from the beginning my goal. Why? It was the only way to prove that a united Cyprus conscience, which is necessary to unite the sides, does not exist within the masses. If we are all Cypriots, Turks and Greeks on the island, then why was my documentary labeled as a one-sided project? Why was the suffering of the "one" never mentioned by the "other"? Why was my documentary rejected not only from the Greek side but also by many pro-Greek Turkish Cypriots? Why on earth am I a traitor? The answer for me lays in one fact. We have on the island four basic categories of people: Greek, Turkish, Pro-Greek, pro-Turkish, but a very small minority of pro-Cypriots who can make the difference.

So if there is no Cypriot conscience, which is possible to unite the people, why all the effort? You don't go to war because you know you are going to win, you go because it's your duty to defend your family and country. You don't say I will die so I won't go. Responsibility is what takes you to the battle field, and the righteousness of your cause provides you the hope of victory. Your loved ones are so important that you stand, and the only thing you can say is, "if I perish, I perish".

My intention in this book is not to analyze in depth the Cyprus problem, or attempt to throw blame one side or the other for the past conflicts between Greek and Turkish Cypriots, although I can point out mistakes done from both sides very easily. If the past is worth looking into, it's only to acknowledge our mistakes so we won't repeat them in the future and to apologize where needed, thus transforming them into bridges of reconciliation with the other side. I admit though that my target from the beginning was the Greek community from where I have my roots.

The reason for this was the impact the subject had on my personal life and the positive changes it brought in me. I was a Greek nationalist myself, worse of the kind, a Turk-hater plus a communist- hater. The realities I had discovered destroyed my national arrogance, and forced me to reconsider many of my one-sided beliefs. The hate

12

in me brought on by national duty was revealed and destroyed, and then love and understanding prevailed. I was born again!

Of course when I use the word "mistakes" in the above paragraph it is important to understand that this word is easily used by politicians in a general way that can mean anything, not always something unethical. Unfortunately the past mistakes made by Cypriots were not limited to misestimated policies but was also expanded to crimes, causing the death of many innocent people either because of their political views, or their national identity. Some lost their lives just because they were in the wrong place at the wrong time. Families that have been victims of such crimes have a tendency to follow extreme nationalist groups either from fear or from anger. Fear because of the psychological trauma they have experienced, anger because the crimes went unpunished.

Once someone tries to dig the past in search for more light into the island's recent history (1960-74), he is walking on very thin ice. This is for two main reasons: One is the fact that people involved in such crimes are still alive and for obvious reasons they don't want to be exposed. Secondly and probably most significant is the fact that today's politics are in continuity with the past; hence any recognition of past faults threatens the foundations of current policies. For this reason strong propaganda machines are working overtime not only to prove to the rest of the world that their side is right, but also to hide their wrong doings from view of their own communities. To achieve this, the leaders must have control of the sources from which the people are receiving information, the media and the education system.

With the education system, it is much easier because schools are mainly government institutions, so history books were and are manipulated accordingly, though in the North the last few years history books have had positive changes. Having circulated in quite a few schools in my childhood and with my three children today in primary and high school, I know from first hand knowledge how the system works and I accept no argument in the matter. Just very recently my eldest daughter, age 17, was rebuked strongly by a teacher because she wrote on her school sack, "Turkish Cypriots are my brothers". When she changed school middle of the first semester, she was welcomed with a threat by a classmate that saw the same text on her sack. A few months earlier she was brutally beaten by a nationalist gang that attacked leftist youth in a summer camp in Larnaca district because they said they had betrayed the EOKA cause and insulted general Grivas (EOKA leader).

With the media, although they are private organizations, it wasn't hard to handle because almost nobody would dare to stand against his own nationals, thus be called a traitor by the majority, especially in times of communal conflicts. In the past a few journalists who had the nerve to do so, paid a high price, some even with their own lives. Newspaper "Politis" that was pro-yes during the referendum came under great pressure and the journalists credibility was openly attacked by the government. The newspaper was sued for almost anything in an attempt to be silenced.

Knowing all this, somebody may ask, why did I step out from the crowd and put my self in that dangerous position of becoming a traitor and live under constant threat? Am I an eccentric weirdo, as some have suggested? Maybe I am! Which eccentric weirdo would acknowledge that anyway? Everybody likes to think of himself as a normal person living amongst eccentrics. That's probably the reason we don't have so many real friends in our lifetime. We are trying to connect with people that are exactly like us, but there are not two people that match exactly on this earth, and probably this is the beauty of life. Each and every one of us is a unique musical instrument that echoes his distinctive melody. Together we construct the world's orchestra that makes the universe rock.

So based on my philosophy I cannot judge if I am eccentric but I can only speak about my idiosyncrasy. Four words motivate my life: Freedom, Righteousness, Truth and Peace. The fundamental lie of the lazy, the cowards, and the ones in a position of gaining from the status quo, is that the world can not change, so why bother? But if you look a few years back, you can see hundreds of changes in the world. Let me point out some.

1. The checkpoints in Cyprus have opened.
2. The Berlin wall is not there any more.
3. The iron curtain has fallen.
4. Turkish Cypriots are not in enclaves.
5. Workers work only 8 hours a day.
6. Nazism was overcome and Europe rebuilt.
7. The skeleton figures in Auschwitz erected a country.
8. The French aristocracy has fallen.
9. The British Empire has fallen.
10. The Ottoman Empire has fallen.
11. The Popes Inquisition is not in effect.

The list can go for many pages. Did our grandfathers have TV sets, or even imagine the possibility of traveling with iron birds through the skies, or that a city could vanish within minutes by a single bomb? The world has changed and it will go on changing. Change is the only constant thing. The issue is what direction it will take. That's up to us to decide. Many will argue that it's the politicians that shape the world. Yes, but again I ask, who votes them into position?

Am I a man of extra courage, as some have suggested? Of course not! I love life to its fullest and have four children who I want to see growing up. I have the same fears as all human beings, but maybe what makes me do what I do is love, not courage. I love my country and my children too much to sit back and do nothing. Real love is never considering what it can get but what it can give. The matter is to love enough not to give up, because it's in such times as this that we must plant our feet firmer in the ground and claim peace and reconciliation.

It's also a matter of conscience. Better die younger but sleep peacefully at night, without having those voices chasing me around chastising my soul. For some people to keep quiet is easy. They think that by silencing their conscience they have less responsibility, but deep inside they are tormented by their choice to keep silent. I have my fears, but I crucified my fears on the cross of responsibility. Maybe if I knew the power of the stream I would have never swam against it, but now it's too late. I have jumped in the current and I must go all the way. As poet Robert Frost said, *"Two roads diverged in a wood and I took the one less traveled by and that made all the difference."*

We will never change our world intimidated by fear or disappointment. We must at least try to transcend above those negative psychologies that freezes our spirit, and act. The Cyprus problem did not start with the Annan Plan and it does not stop with it either. The plan is not as important as reconciliation is. Any plan can be effectively accepted by both communities, as was the Zurich-London agreements, and be canceled with the first chance. But even the worst of plans can be preserved if the hearts are in the right place. I believe that if we don't build bridges of understanding and reconciliation, any plan is bound to fail anyway. This is where the focus must be rather than on scattered ideas. If hatred is hanging around, a solution will never be solid.

To be honest, though I don't like to act as a prophet, I believe that even if all the changes in the Annan Plan requested by Papadopoulos are accepted by the Turkish Cypriot leadership, there will still be no solution. I am not a nihilist, but it's obvious that the problem goes deeper than what's been claimed. Just the fact that to come to the point of referendum so many conjunctions had to come together is something that needs to ponder us. Why do we need these conjunctions? Is it because in reality the two communities are walking on different paths? Is it because they have no self will and have become a prey to the policies of superior powers? But the supreme question is when will our planets meet again?

Today the island's future lies in the hands of the new generation of Cypriots. Politicians and journalists are in a position that can reach the masses. What would their message be, hatred or reconciliation, unity or division?

There is a universal principle that says, "What you sow you will also reap". Maybe some of you don't believe that the two communities must unite. Division can also be a solution but you must understand that even with such a solution, peace and reconciliation must prevail with the neighboring state, otherwise our children may have the same end as the children of Murataǧa (Maratha). You may say this is not possible. Do you think those spreading the seeds of hatred a century ago imagined that one day the island would be over-crowded with mass graves?

· PREFACE

*"The dead cannot cry out for justice;
it is a duty of the living to do so for them"*
Lois McMaster Bujold

They asked me many times why I picked the old scabs and would not leave the past to be forgotten. The answer is easy. The scabs are not old. If they were that old we would not have the mothers in black, the guns, armies, barriers.

Although I have lived for forty years in this island, I am newly discovering the other half of the truth. When I reflect on the wall of propaganda that my society has erected deliberately to hide half of the truth, the past turns into a frightening today. Suddenly you understand that you have to dig up the soil with your bare hands until they bleed in order to find the missing truth. If you speak out they will call you a traitor. You may even be threatened with death. Your friends may turn against you. You can end up alone.

Being alone does not frighten me any more. A lot of the children of Murataga have been climbing onto my bed at night for some time. We read stories together. They smile because I am telling their stories to the world. And I am crying my eyes out as they leave before I get to count the bullet holes in their tiny bodies. Their wounds must be fresh because when I

19

wake up I find fresh red blood stains on my white sheet. Their wounds must most certainly be fresh because nobody has apologized for them yet.

This book is dedicated to the Murataga, Sandallar and Atlılar Primary School children who were killed and buried in a mass grave in 1974.

If only a simple apology could be enough...

Tony Angastiniotis

PART -I-
VOICE OF BLOOD

"No army can withstand the strength
of an idea whose time has come."

Victor Hugo

This short book is a guidebook to my experiences which have stamped themselves upon me and my family forever. It is related to my research and my documentary about Turkish Cypriots being murdered by Greek Cypriots in August 1974.

The filming of "the Voice of Blood" documentary started in August 2004 and was completed in the same month. In this thirty minute documentary I recorded the statements of people who escaped the massacres committed by Greek-Cypriots in the villages of Murataga, Sandallar, Atlılar and Tohni. What rates this documentary different from others is that a Greek for the first time records the other side of the coin.

The time at which the documentary was prepared and presented by the media had an importance in itself. It was at the time following the referendum about the acceptance of the Annan Plan. Greek Cypriots were divided into two as the "yes-men" and the "no-men", patriots and traitors, those who accepted bribes from the Americans and those who did not. At the same time, young Turkish Cypriots, following their "Yes" revolution, had fallen from the clouds due to the disillusionment brought by the Greek Cypriots' "No," which left them in the status quo. To all these was added the Talat government crisis, as an early election had to take place because his party had lost the majority vote.

Out of the indefinite state of affairs which was dominant on both sides, grew a documentary which aimed to address both communities, although it presented the crimes committed by only one side. This documentary was a shock for the Greek Cypriot community, and a blow to their nationalist pride which had reached a peak after the referendum. The Olympics in Athens and winning the European Football Cup were effective in raising their nationalistic feelings.

The documentary shows the mass-murder of women, children and the elderly-victims of the Greeks. Suddenly everything is turned upside down. The Greek Cypriots who claimed to be the only victims in 1974 became the villains. Are there any omitted events that we are not aware of? Is part of our history hidden from us? Why have these crimes been covered up?

How can one be proud of these crimes? How innocent are we as Greeks? These are two questions that come to the mind of the average civilian.

On the other hand, the situation was very different on the Turkish Cypriot side. These crimes were all too familiar to them. They only learned couple of extra details in this documentary. What was important was the fact that for the first time a Greek was telling their drama objectively to his own people. A Greek addressed Turkish Cypriots as brothers, shared their sorrow at a time of tension between Turks and Greeks, during the big OXI (NO) vote in the referendum. This was no empty slogan. This was love which was crystallised by a work of art - the documentary. It was also a challenge of courage. Could the Turkish side also accept their crimes? Will they allow a Greek to show more courage than them? Could they also hang out their dirty laundry for all to see?

Should both sides find themselves able to confess fully to past crimes, this could only do a power of good for both communities. Whatever the politicians might do, they cannot change the human aspect of this story. They cannot make their legalistic excuses. The crimes go way beyond the legal complications of the Cyprus problem; they strike at the heart. Crimes were committed, and no one was held accountable. People were murdered, families wiped out. Who can deny the truth?

It has become clear that many Greeks consider me a traitor because of the content of my documentary. Patriots are not supposed to tell such truths. To the Greek mind, Cyprus is Greek and will remain Greek. Crimes committed by Turks were the acts of barbarians, while the acts of the Greeks were justified under the conditions of the times.

A journalist from the *Simerini* newspaper, who saw me on T.V as a guest of Bayrak Television, asked, "Can there be a Greek who hates his own people so much?" He wrote of me that I had started a smear campaign in order to "open the Doors of Rage." This person, needless to say, does not know me. Nor did he consult me before putting ink to page. However, I agree with him on one point. I'm opening the Doors of Rage consciously and with no regrets. I am playing my last card for my divided country.

Simerini journalists ask, "Where shall we begin?" Shall we start from 1974, 1963, 1958, or from the beginning of the century? We could, of course, start from long before that. For example, from Tripolitsa where Greeks massacre 20,000 Turkish women and children, including the Jewish population in three days. But we had better not go that far back lest they call us backward in our thinking.

So we shall talk about the Greeks murdered in Kondemenos in 1958, but as good Greeks we are not going to mention the Turkish Cypriots killed in Sinta. We will say that fifty-six Greek Cypriots were killed in clashes in '58 but we won't mention the fifty-three Turks who were killed at this time - otherwise we would be opening the Doors of Rage. I had better not mention 1963; otherwise the people who are lying in mass graves in Ayios Vassillios will haunt us.

Then we will come to 1974 and talk about Assia, Palekithro, Trimithi - but not mention for one minute Murataǧa, Sandallar, Atlılar, Tohni, Alamino. This would not serve our political propaganda purposes at all. Denying these atrocities however, will not help to bring peace either.

Therefore I am opening the Doors of Rage, and therefore I want us to face the realities of our history. Let us uncover the truth until we can see everything; and until we can face our guilt and face ourselves. What I ask from both communities is to listen to the sufferings and concerns of one another. Rather than a warm

24

embrace between the people, we have had the cold embrace of the mass grave. In both societies women became widows, mothers lost their children, children became orphans, and babies sucked blood. We cannot take this pain away from the victims. I believe that we should lift up the carpet and clean out the dirt that is concealed there.

For neither side is there a short route to purification. A mother or a father who has lost a child, or a woman who has lost her husband, cannot very easily walk across the bridges of reunification of the island. Not all Greeks are murderers, nor are all Turks. However, we who form the majority have become the victims of the psychopathic minds of those who seek to kill off our friendship. We have to oppose this hatred and bitterness in order to build a better future for our children, and to build firm foundations for their homeland.

One of the questions I often come across is, "Why did you prepare a documentary which presents the concerns of only one side?" This is not a difficult question to answer. I can answer it with another question. Which is the "other side" if we call the Turkish Cypriots brothers? When did the Greek side ever share the Turkish side's pain - or vice versa? Maybe never until the day I found the boldness to produce "Voice of Blood." During this undertaking I felt as if I were being purified from my racist identity. My "enemy's" pain became my pain. I identified with his pain as a fellow human made of the same material, dust. This means that my enemy will also reach the same conclusion - if he can approach the matter with the same objectivity. He will feel my pain. If everybody could do this, the whole concept of enmity would have been evaporated.

But wait. What on earth will our politicians do over the next forty years? Will they find themselves compelled at last to deal with boring subjects such as economic development, prosperity for the country? Most politicians are not economists anyway, they are advocates. Tension and conflict is in their very nature. They want to win the arguments even if they don't know what they are talking about. If my lawyer was unable to find a solution to my problems in forty years time, I would sack him. He must be either incompetent or unwilling to solve the problem.

Our lawyer-politicians are never guilty in Cyprus. It is always the opposite party who is unwilling to compromise. According to one side, Denktaş is the guilty man. The other side contends it is the Greeks who cannot face up to their crimes. Greeks say "Greeks cannot live with Turks." There is a saying that if you bury the truth a thousand lies will sprout from the soil. I have Turkish friends in Cyprus and Istanbul - and we get on very well. We have never had a fight. Not one.

Papandreou dances Zeibekiko with them, Karamanlis signs as best man in their weddings. When there is an earthquake we run to the ruins to help them. How is it that we claim that we cannot live together? Maybe we do not want to - but that's a different story.

The peace process in Cyprus has opened up new horizons for me. I am sure others from our bi-communal society will likewise be enlightened. There is a tide flowing in the press which even the political establishment will find difficult to control. Sevgül Uludağ has researched crimes documented in the Yeni Düzen and Alithia newspapers, and she has publicized them. Marios Dimitriou has done the same thing in Alithia newspaper; Şener Levent is pushing his society in this direction. Even Lazaros Mavros, known for his strong nationalistic opinions, has called for an inquiry into the Tohni murders. He asked the Attorney General in an article called *Tohni* to institute such an inquiry in Simerini newspaper (24-25 October, and again 10 November 2004). His implication that I am among "the ones who are trying to blame the Greeks for the murders" is not so important. What is important is that the spark has caught.

This documentary may never be shown on Greek channels. Nevertheless, the darkness of the past has been slightly illuminated, if not through television then through the written word.

After completing the documentary, I did not go back to the south. Nor, for that matter, did I stay in the north. My life was suddenly trapped in the green line. My heart instinctively shunned the degradation of hatred planted by other generations, centuries ago. My mind rejected the idea of teaching such hatred to my own children, the hatred that blighted my childhood.

I soon realized that it was not only me who was trapped in the green line. Hundreds of Turkish and Greek Cypriots were trapped there among the minefields of various periods, the bloody barbed wire. They were trapped in the ruins of the Dead Zone. It is easy to differentiate the ones trapped there. Usually they have two mobile phones. One is for speaking with their friends in the south, the other for speaking with their friends in the north. This is clear evidence that a lot of people have learned the language of peace, and that they speak it fluently.

Its amazing how mobile phones and emails don't acknowledge the existence of borderlines.

PART -II-
SEARCHING FOR THE TRUTH

"Men occasionally stumble over the truth,
but most of them pick themselves up
and hurry off as if nothing ever happened."
Winston Churchill

Peace did indeed come to us - but already it is
departing. Politicians continue their fights against the
people who want to be relieved of the burden brought by
the hatred of their forefathers.

The 1960's generation is still enthroned and has
blazing rows, the nature of which we do not understand,
or want to understand. We ask to live in peace and
in harmony, like brothers. All we want is this. But I
do not say everyone wants the same thing, even those of
the younger generation. What I mean is that the cultured
among us want peace and harmony. But let me make
myself clear about this. Being educated and being
cultured are two different things. A few days ago I met a
metal worker on a construction site. He did not have a
great vocabulary, and he had trouble expressing himself.
However, it was obvious that his thoughts were of a
highly cultured nature.

Those who meet me wonder whether I am left wing
or right wing. Anyone who gets onto my case asks me
this question. It is only Sener Levent who asked me this
question of which wing I belonged to before finding out

anything else about me. But really, how can you wish to limit an eagle, used to having the range of the skies, to the area of a cage? I am an internationalist - and therefore I own the whole sky, the whole universe. If a Turk is in pain, then so am I. If a Greek is in pain, then so am I. I show the same sensitivity towards the left wing and the right wing. If it is communism which is oppressing a country I shout "Communism out!" If it is capitalism which is oppressing the people, I shout "Capitalism out!"

In my opinion people are not to be categorized according to their political flavors, nationalities or religious beliefs. They are only to be categorized as pro-violence or peacemakers. I choose pro-peace people but I love also the pro-war people. I understand their illness, and I struggle in my laboratory of dialogue to find a suitable form of treatment.

It is not easy in a small society like Cyprus where everybody knows everyone to erase the label of traitor. The political instability under which Cyprus has been languishing for so long has facilitated a propaganda machine that can cut people' down in record time. If you can endure like Jonah 3 days in the belly of the fish, maybe you can find again the way to Nineveh and accomplish your task.

I believe that in order to fully understand what happened between Turkish and Greek Cypriots, to understand all the violence, one must first listen to the witnesses' testimony; then compare both sides' accounts, test them against the archives and try not to put the nationalistic blinders on while doing so. My search began on the internet, developed through historical archives, and ended with live witnesses.

The stories I heard about the barbarisms against the Turks of Cyprus shocked me the most for two reasons. Firstly, I was taught since childhood that only the Turks had committed crimes in Cyprus. Secondly, the effectiveness of the Greek Cypriot propaganda machine in burying unpalatable truths deep beneath the ground. Maybe Turkish propaganda is the same, although I have not come across it yet. I should be charitable, but I have not said that the Turks are innocent. What I do say is that the barbarism of Greeks affects me more as I have been brought up with the idea that "those who are not Hellenes are barbarians." Or to put it another way, all Hellenes are pure.

There was one inescapable factor in my research into the crimes of the past forty years. And it was not to do with the crimes of the 1960s, but of 1974. It was the mass murders carried out in Muratağa, Sandallar, Atlılar and Tohni. What made these crimes so terrible was the way in which the victims were murdered as well as their ages. They were all women, children and elderly. They were not the sort who would have been able to fight. And even if they had been capable of resistance, it's not part of the game to murder unarmed people. If you are a legal state you should play the game in an honest manner according to its rules. Just like Caesar's wife. It is, of course, important which Caesar we are talking about. Julius, Augustus or Caligula?

As the father of four children I could not but sympathize with the pain of Turkish Cypriot fathers who came back from internment camps to find their wives,

31

children, mothers and fathers killed. What would I do if I found, for example, someone from my family burnt or decapitated when I arrived home from work? As a human being, how can one be indifferent to such pain, whatever the nationality of the victim?

My first thought was, hang on a minute, is it even remotely possible that Greeks could commit such crimes? What if the evidence is merely the product of the Turkish propaganda machine - churned out to justify the intervention of the Turks in 1974, and to cover up the crimes that the Turks had committed?

I was only eight years old during the events of 1974. Turkish planes were bombing extensively and my childish mind was affected by the noise. While everyone was trying to run and hide, I was most eager to see the planes from the window.

I asked several friends to get me some information about the events of 1974. No one could remember very much. My mother remembered what happened because she was in England at that time, and had watched the digging up of mass graves on the BBC. She said to me, half in Greek, half in English:

-    I remember some things but not the details.

-    My dear mom, I need details because I have set out to save Cyprus on my own.

And in a flash a voice inside me shouted "Andreas Parashos." How on earth did I not think of him before? I had worked at ALPHA TV with Andreas, and I recalled that he had conducted research concerning the missing

32

Greek Cypriots who were buried in Lakatamia cemetery. (Many Greek Cypriots who were missing in action from 1974 were buried in Lakatamia cemetery without their families been notified.)

I did not call Andreas. I just went to Politis newspaper and appeared in his office rather like a parachutist from a clear sky. Fortunately, he received me as if we had an appointment set up a century ago.

I read Andreas' column "Parteri" in Politis newspaper every day. Thus I knew that our views were identical. I do not mean this in terms of being left wing or right wing. Such things are in the past. I am always fond of journalists like Andreas who put their views forward openly. Writers like Andreas help those who do not know what to think to open up their minds to facts and to new horizons.

Andreas listened to me very carefully. I was talking to him while at the same time crying like a child whose toy has been taken from him. I felt like a deceived spouse who has just found out that the relationship he thought he had is a lie. At the heart of the state that I had supported passionately for years lived bloodthirsty murderers, killers of babies. The state would send poor people who could not pay their bills to prison, but did nothing to punish those murderers. I begged him, "Tell me Andreas," (crying), "tell me that it's not true! Tell me that I am a victim of Turkish propaganda, and that this nightmare will end."

After listening to me for ten to fifteen minutes, Andreas put his pipe down and opened the file in front of him, as if he had known I was going to visit him and had prepared for it. Damn it! Were his eyes full of tears too? There were other documents in the file as well as pictures of missing Turkish Cypriots.

"Andreas, I want to do something for this country but I'm an ordinary citizen - what can I do?"
"Carry on doing what you're already doing."

"Yes, but what should I do then?"

"Carry on," he repeated, and sent me away by entrusting me to God. This is what Andreas is like. He shows you a direction and... find it if you can. If you have it in you, and if you can put up with the pressure, you can find the light. Otherwise, at least the smell of his pipe lingers.

Andreas had photographs and documents. In other words, this was his message: There was truth in the story of the Murataǧa mass graves.

I sat at the computer and searched the internet for foreign media coverage of the mass graves. I sat there all night. In the morning I went to the Archbishopric archive department and had a look at the Greek press. I even tried to get some information from a sweet old lady working at the kiosk there. I thought, as she was old she must have seen a lot. But all I learned from her was the secrets of her life. "I'm the archbishop's sister but I haven't had a penny from the wealth of the church." Now this is what I called honesty! She must have been telling the truth. If she had taken money from the church, she would not have been working at that kiosk selling fruit juice. (There was a scandal at this time about relatives of the Archbishop and church land.)

The research I did at the Archbishopric archive and the internet helped to lighten up the dark tunnel of history.

FILELEFTHEROS
3rd September 1974

PROPAGANDA NOISES FROM TURKS FINDING MASS GRAVES - GOVERNMENT SUGGESTS RESEARCH COMMITTEE

The state spokesperson made the following explanation:

It has been seen as necessary to clarify matters in relation to the assertion that a mass grave of Turkish Cypriots has been found in Murataǧa. In the area where this mass grave has been found there are hundreds of Greeks missing. An object found on a dead woman's body retrieved from the mass grave is in the possession of the government. The object leads us to think its owner is Greek. (The object was a medallion with a picture of the Parthenon).

There is an explanation from UNIFCYP in the same article:

35

Last night 20 corpses, mostly children, were uncovered. Identification cannot be achieved because the bodies are badly burnt.

FILELEFTHEROS
4th September 1974

THEY CLAIM MASSACRE IN TOHNI.
ALL MISSING TURKS CONSIDERED TO BE MASSACRED.

In the article the state spokesperson says this:

The Turks, with the hope that they will distract the attention of the public from the terrible effects of the invasion in Cyprus, are claiming again that they are tracing another mass grave in another area The government said that it will assist United Nations efforts to conduct an examination of the area in question.

MAHI
5th September 1974

The State spokesperson answered a question as to whether it was true or not that RMMO had tried to stop the UN searching for a mass grave in the Palodia Village, and said that RMMO insists that these examinations should be made in the Turkish areas as well as in the Greek areas.

Owner of *Mahi* was Nikos Sampson. He was declared president by the Greek junta during the coup d'etat, on the 15th of July 1974 that led to the Turkish intervention five days later.

I must also be objective and say that no Turkish newspaper admitted any Greek killings during the war.

AP Reporter David Lancashire

"A mass grave, in which more than 80 Turkish Cypriot men, women and children were buried, has been exhumed on the outskirts of the village of Murataga. This is the greatest atrocity committed against the civilians, which has been discovered after the cessation of the war in Cyprus."

Reported by CBS Television

"Corpses of 88 Turkish Cypriots have been discovered on a rubbish heap, in Nicosia. These people had been gunned down by the Greek Cypriots and Greeks and before their murder they had been tied up with wire. The heads of some of the corpses had been severed form the bodies."

Reported by Sun newspaper

"I saw the Murataga calamity. The interpretation of such barbaric action can be different, but apart form saying that a savage murder has been committed in Murataga, what else can be said?"

AFP Reporter Bernard Nicholas

"Bodies of Turkish Cypriots who have been murdered by Greek Cypriots have been exhumed form a mass-grave in the village of Atlılar"

The newspapers of the period testified to the presence of mass graves in Tohni and Murataǧa. What should I do now?

PART -III-
THE BIG DECISION

"Be realistic, demand the impossible"
Ernesto Che Guevera

A friend of mine was going to meet a Turkish Cypriot businessman on a Saturday morning. My instinct, that inner soft voice that rises from our gut, said "go with him."

Metin has a factory in the Nicosia industrial estate. He has business relations with a lot of Greeks. His office was the messiest I have ever seen in my life. In the room at the front of his office there were metal samples and papers. We found space to sit down after rearranging the detritus of his office. I thought, "It was a mistake to come. At least I have seen what a factory owner's office looks like. A mess!"

With increasing embarrassment I sat amid the chaos of the room when I spotted two big books standing in the corner. They looked like albums. Meanwhile, people would keep coming and going and we would exchange a couple of words. My mind was on those two books. Should I go and open them? I could not decide. What if they contained private matters? But then, if I had the power to resist curiosity, why would I conduct research in the first place? I stood up and approached the books like a cold-blooded executioner, to murder my reluctance without shame. They were full of newspapers from the 1960s. Metin was interested in history, and he was an active member of a political party. He had even stood as a candidate at one of the elections. My intuition had found me a base upon which to stand.

It was time for my attack. Timing was very important. I could miss the train easily, but that carriage could not have gone without me. I told Metin about my research and he told me that he knew a Turkish Cypriot whose cousin had survived the mass murders in Tohni. He telephoned him immediately and made an appointment for two days hence.

On 28th June 2004, at lunch-time my wife Christiana and my daughter Nefeli accompanied me to the village of Vouno - what is now called Taşkent. It sits under the flag drawn up by the Turks on the Pendadaktylos /Beşparmak mountain range. What the witness Suat Hüseyin told us was very breath-taking and we will examine it in the following chapter. This was when I decided to go one step further than writing a book and to prepare a documentary. I was not sure how I would do it without any money or equipment, but I knew that I would do it because the drive to do it was so very strong.

When I got home I phoned a very good friend of mine, a cameraman, and shared my idea with him. As I knew him well I did not believe he would accept my proposal. However, he surprised me by showing enthusiasm for the project - at least at that moment. As time is money and as I do not often encounter money, I met him the next day and arranged to talk about the shootings. We agreed that I would make all the arrangements.

I immediately got in touch with the Turkish Cypriot Press and Information Office via e-mail, and we agreed to meet Mr. Mustafa Erülgen as soon as he came back from a ten-day leave. This gave me enough time to look into the events in question and plan the logistics. I was so lost in my research that my family started to become worried about me. The only subject I talked about for weeks was mass graves. I succeeded in steering every subject into the Tohni, Murataǧa and Atlılar events, and the clashes of 1963, until such a time as no one would want to speak to me. I became monotonous. I became boring.

I carried on reading books about witnesses of the period in question, and going through the old newspapers in the Archbishopric archive. The rest of the time I spent talking to anyone who had experienced the events of the 1960s and 1974. Information from ordinary people gave me the clearest image of what Cyprus was like in those days. But one particular problem soon emerged. Once I had announced that I was writing a book, most people concerned decided that they did not want their names mentioned, and they became extremely camera shy. I tried to convince my wife's uncle for forty minutes to do an interview on camera, but he did not accept, even if we concealed his identity.

The demons of nationalism are still around us, and they are still sucking our blood. It is hard to find people willing to go against these demons. Only someone like me could go against them. Someone told me to simply let it be. "They will laugh at you as they might laugh at a messianic lunatic in the streets." But pressing on was of such overriding importance that one could call it an effort towards salvation. I want to live free from the

hatred and discord which gnawed at our grandfathers'
bodies and now gnaw at ours.

Those around me thought me on the point of losing
my marbles. Most still see me like this. What I saw were
the bullet wounds in the Murataǧa children. I would
wake up with the screams of the execution. It felt as
though I were the one pulling the trigger and as if my
children were the ones being murdered. I cursed my
rich imagination. I could see the trigger finger close
up at the same time as I saw the bullet rip into a
mother via the body of her child. I had to make
that documentary as soon as possible, otherwise the
nightmares would continue.

One or two days before meeting Mustafa the phone
rang rather strangely. I know it when the phone rings
strangely as there is a knot in my stomach and I am
disinclined to answer it. I feel like this when the bank
calls me. At the other end of the phone was my
cameraman friend. Our dialogue was more or less like
this:

-Hey Tony, I've changed my mind.
-Why's that, mate?
-I'm scared. I've got a family. You don't know "them"
very well. We'll be found in a ditch somewhere.
-But who are "they"?
-The nationalists who control the country mate. You
don't know what happened at the referendum - that's
why you talk. I was involved in things, I saw a lot.
You'd better give it all up, don't be crazy.
-Why are you afraid? We live in a republic.
-You mean a banana republic. You've seen what was
done to Anastasiadis (they threw a grenade at him) - you

want the same thing to happen to you? They drew a list of the people voting yes. Times have changed. I'm your friend and I've warned you. But do as you please.

I thought this through. If my friend was right, then it might be time to test and to try our democracy. It might be time to see what our government and our public are made of. I could not accept being scared into silence, could not accept a policy of fear in a democratic country. If such a policy existed, it would need to be uncovered. Yet one thing was clear. I would have to proceed alone.

My wife was conducting her own struggle with the newborn child at her breast. She was also frightened that I was in danger. "You're having another Che Guevera attack and trying to save the world." I am not sure how I managed to convince her that one can only change the world by believing in one's aims, but somehow I did. If your partner will not fight by your side, you cannot go to war. I often sang this line of a song to her - "from your love, I will take the power to conquer the whole word." She thought I was joking.

When had I finished the documentary and came home with the master copy in my hand, we hugged each other. She was probably thinking "He's done it, the loony." Our cheeks stuck to each other with sweat and tears. I never loved a woman as I loved her.

A while later an August noontime turned as cold as a January night. My brain had started to work. At that time we were both aware of the hard road we were on, and the challenges we were to face.

While sitting on a bench in Girne some days later I noticed my wife looking at me with those big black eyes that captured my heart one summer. "What are you thinking?" I asked.

"I'm wondering why you can't be a normal human being. You know, a normal man with a decent salary who doesn't try to change the world."

"I try to be like that, but I can't help myself. My mind asks the same question to my heart every day, but my heart remains silent. It's also to do with conscience...but I still haven't worked out how the system inside me works."

Consulting many people at this time, one signal came in most clearly. "Don't go against Tassos Papadopoulos [the Greek president] or he will eat you for breakfast." For the first time I felt fear. The people telling me this were from the sixties generation, the time of the cannibals, and they knew a few things. I had nightmares in which I was being turned over a fire like a piglet on a spit. Gathered around were Tassos and his ministers discussing my progress and deciding what to spread over my half burnt skin.

In the end, this is the problem in Cyprus. Everyone is frightened of being barbecued. Terrible events took place when Defkalion (this was Papadopoulos' code name in EOKA) and the left wing clashed, and

44

comrades were stoned in the streets. But what has all this got to do with our era? The comrades and Defkalion made peace, and they have become brothers. We are now a European country. We can express our selves freely.

I wish to explain something so that I will not be misunderstood. What makes me angry is not Tassos and his government. There have been five other governments who have ignored what was done to the Turkish Cypriots. The fact is that murderers on a grand scale have not been hunted down and turned over to the courts for the simple fact that their victims were of another religion. This shows a clear democratic deficit in our country. What on earth is the meaning of a legal government which discriminates against its own people?

None of the Greeks who committed war crimes were ever handed over to justice. I am not a one-man court. I am simply passing on the truth as it appears to me. I am also trying to understand the mentality behind these events with whatever capacity for logic God has given me.

PART -IV-
CROSSING THE BARRICADES

"If you want to make peace, you don't talk to your friends. You talk to your enemies."

Moshe Dayan

I crossed the green line at 9:30 on a hot August morning. We do not recognize Turkish Cypriot state, but we fill in visa forms and we show our passports. In the casinos at night, Greek is spoken everywhere. Our taxi drivers have one year car insurance for the North as they cross regularly for cheap petrol.

Relieved of three Cyprus pounds for the taxi ride, we went to the Information Bureau where I would meet Mustafa. Mustafa Erulgen is quite tall, dark skinned, short haired and a bit overweight, as befits a man of consequence in the state. Despite my misgivings at his stern demeanor, I soon found myself received with great kindness and interest. Mustafa asked about my plans for the documentary, and wanted to know when we would start shooting. Poor man, I thought, he probably sees me like a BBC producer, laden with the latest equipment, come to make the big documentary about the Turkish Cypriots. It was my fault, of course. I had come to his office with an "I'm going to save the world" attitude.

Come on, I told myself. Convince the man of your poverty and ask for some equipment. Meanwhile,

Mustafa was looking into my eyes in an indecisive manner. I thought to myself, my dear Tony get ready to be kicked out, you are trying to sell lizards for anchovies to the wrong customer. He carried on looking at me. He was probably wondering whether this mad Greek could possible make an objective documentary on the subject of mass graves. He must have been in quite a dilemma because he was tapping his foot fast and rhythmically, swiveling his chair from left to right. He looked into my eyes and then at my tattoo covering my left arm with hieroglyphics. The inevitable question comes to mind. What serious person covers his arms with tattoos?

I acquired those tattoos one August day when I was a young boy on holiday in Paphos. I dipped a needle into ink and feverishly jabbed holes in my skin like one demented. I seem to do all the mad things of my life in August. Perhaps it is the heat.

Mustafa suddenly stood up and told me to follow him to the director's room. I hate the words director, head etc. When I was in high school I would pop into the headmaster's room almost every day to listen to sermons about my behavior. Those visits continued until one of the teachers called me a donkey and I pinned him to the wall and wouldn't let go until he called me "Mr. Tony". This was to be my last scholastic experience, and I checked out then and there. I left my schoolbag behind, carrying a greater burden instead, working in a petrol station at day and rushing every evening to night school.

The director's desk was eight meters long. It was a bit too long for the small young man sitting at it. The fact that Hüseyin Özel was so young impressed me. I thought bravo Talat. He gave responsibility to young progressive people with wide perspectives by kicking the old ones out. This country can only progress by doing such things. I have respect for old people. We need their experience and advice, but the future belongs not to the ones who are going but to the ones who are coming.

Hüseyin Özel listened to my arguments with care. I told him that I had once been extremely right wing. What I found out while searching through history rescued my soul from the illness of nationalist racism. If faced with these facts, other citizens could also be rescued. In the end Hüseyin was convinced that I was indeed trying to promote peace, and this was the key to our cooperation.

I knew that, like most of Talat's men, he was in the peace camp, and wanted a solution to the Cyprus problem passionately. Even Talat at one meeting gave me some advice which I thought only a Greek could possibly come out with. I wonder if the roles had changed, and that I had failed to notice it? Maybe it had always been like that without my having noticed it. Who can understand what is happening on this island amongst all this polemical propaganda?

Hüseyin picked up the phone and talked to the BRT television studio. At the other end of the line another Hüseyin volunteered to help. They would give us a final answer in a couple of days.

I left satisfied that I had convinced them all, but also in a maze of thoughts all leading to a great fear. I had long known that my course of action would affect my family and my own well being. I had struggled with myself, had thought of giving up, but had found that things had grown out of my control. With Christiana quite drained by looking after the baby, I would have to make all my decisions alone. My close friends were unwilling to be involved directly or actively. In short, all responsibility was on my shoulders.

My heart, mind and soul struggled with each other. Cyprus is ill, in discord. It carries the virus of hatred in its veins. This virus must be killed before it infects another generation. If not, we may see our children killing each other - as our fathers killed to exorcise their own pain. This documentary must be an antidote to the poison of discord.

Greeks feel themselves to be the sole victims. They believe they have done nothing to the Turkish Cypriots. If this lie is not destroyed there can never be a real relationship between the two communities. "But the Turks committed terrible crimes in 1974". This is the most popular slogan I hear. I have never denied it. I have seen hundreds of programs, read many books and articles about the barbarism of the Turks. But I have never heard anything about Hellenic barbarism, nor have I read any condemnation of the criminals concerned. I have only heard some left wing slogans - "Turkish Cypriots are our brothers and sisters." Abel was Cain's brother, but when the time came he took him off for a walk and killed him.

What happens if Greeks Cypriots watch a documentary showing the other side of the coin? They will say that I am a traitor, and that I am a Turkish mouthpiece. This is an old trick. All internationalists who have died as traitors have been vindicated. The point is to get the documentary to the general public. In order to do this a sufficient level of democracy is needed. They will say that I am trying to create a general feeling of guilt because of the crimes committed by some EOKA B members. But EOKA B members still have political status and power in Cyprus. They have become ministers, they have become political leaders. They control the tools of mass communication. I am running this campaign only for the sake of this truth. Violence breeds violence and it swells greater each time. The result of this violence is a divided country. If you do not believe this, look at a map of Cyprus. There is a line from Kokkina / Erenkoy to Famagusta, and we will always blame others for the existence of this line.

PART -V-
AT THE SCENE OF THE CRIME

"You're not to be so blind with patriotism that you can't face reality. Wrong is wrong, no matter who does it or says it."

Malcolm X

I met Mustafa at nine in the morning at Kermia checkpoint. We went to the BRT studio, picked up the cameraman and hit the road for Muratağa, Sandallar and Atlılar. Mustafa's presence in the car gave me confidence I might get back home safe and sound.

I checked the map. The villages were somewhere north of the main road to Famagusta, and it looked as if it would take us thirty to forty minutes to get there. I found it difficult to believe that I would at last make my dream come true. I could not keep my mouth shut in the car for all the pent up excitement. Mustafa had to put up with it alone as Savaş the cameraman was sitting in the back fast asleep.

We stopped at Peristeronopigi for a short time. Mud brick houses with big rooms were in a terrible condition, but I liked the place and its feel of the Cyprus of a hundred years ago. From the architecture I guessed that the village was mainly involved in animal husbandry. At one end of the village there was an old run down minaret and a Turkish school. Mustafa told me that they were both knocked down by the Greeks in 1958 during the clashes between the two communities. That was when the Turks left the village. After "independence," Makarios had box-like houses built for them in Murataǧa. Don't get me wrong because I put the word independence in inverted commas. Since the declaration of independence, before I came into existence, nobody has believed in it. Greeks were busy trying to become a province of mainland Greece and the Turks of mainland Turkey. Greece is far away, Turkey is not. Thus, some who had not even heard of the 1960 constitution paid for it with their lives.

After Murataǧa and Sandallar we went to Atlılar. I wanted to have a look around before shooting in order to digest things a little, to get a sense of it all. It was clear that few people were living in those villages. They were abandoned and in ruins. I mentally rebuilt the dilapidated houses, filled the village with crowds and the voices of children. What happened there was a tragedy. A quotation from the Bible came to my mind. Herod orders the massacre of the innocent babies. My eyes were flooding.

"In Rama was there a voice heard,
Lamentation, and weeping, and great mourning,
Rachel weeping for her children,
and would not be comforted, because they are not."
Matthew 2:18

I went to the Atlılar grave with tears in my eyes. On the left hand side on a grey piece of marble these words of Makarios were written. "If Turkey comes to save Turkish Cypriots, she will not find any Turkish Cypriot to save."

I walked towards the slabs where the names were listed, and walked up five steps. I recall that there were five steps for never in my life have I walked up steps with as heavy a heart. Alighting on the fifth step my heart was close to bursting, and I could not hold back my tears. Mustafa and Savaş did not have the heart to come close to me for a while. Guilt and shame embraced me. For those who always knew, this shame was thirty years stale. For me it was fresh. In a sense, those crimes were committed the same day I found out about them, and I have not digested it yet.

I read the names and the ages one by one. I knew the children from my dreams. It was they who called me to document the last days of their lives. My eyes stuck on the name Selden. She was only 16 days old. I immediately thought of my daughter Nefeli. I had seen her in the morning when she was sucking life from her mother's breast. I had thought it impossible to kill a baby on her mother's breast. But if they had let Selden live she would have grown up to become a Turkish mother and give birth to fighters who would then kill Greeks. I cannot think of anything other this idea going through the mind of the one who pulled the trigger. The scamps were applying the ultimate in negative politics.

A white van came and stopped in front of the grave with a sudden jerk. They had probably come to kick us out. They understood from the number plate of our car that a Greek had come to stain the holy place of the martyrs. Mustafa managed to calm then down before they approached me.

Selden's brother, Özmert, pointed out that all the names at the beginning of the list were his relatives. When I looked into Özmert's eyes I saw another crime. This young man had grown up in high drama, had been imprisoned by this cemetery. He had learned about death before he had learned about life. Now, since the checkpoints were opened and Greeks started to cross, he has been the guardian of this holy place.

Mustafa asked Özmert whether his father would do an interview for us. Özmert thought this unlikely. He said journalists had been coming to the village long before, but nothing was ever published on the Greek side. His father found talking about the subject extremely painful, but he, Özmert, would try to convince him, and we should leave our telephone number.

Then we started looking around for people who might be witnesses. But they either did not want to speak to us or were not at home. It was clear from the prevailing atmosphere that the possibility of witnesses giving statements was located between difficult and impossible. We decided to leave the place and come back the next day. Maybe we would be luckier.

On the way back I thought back to when I had cried like that last, and remembered this: I think it was year 1998. I was in front of the prime ministry. I was the cameraman of ALFA channel then. They had sent me to cover Greek President Stefanopoulos talking to missing people relatives. They told us that the Prime minister's car would be at the entrance and the President of Greece would be talking to the relatives. In the end the plan changed and the convoy sped off. The women were disappointed and started to cry. One of them was holding her husband and son's photographs. She threw the photographs onto the ground, and, sobbing, said, "How long are we going to wait?" The glass was all smashed. My heart as well as hers was also smashed up. My hands were shaking. I put the camera down and started crying with her. It was as if her husband was my father and her son my brother.

There is not a flag, language, or race for human pain. It is internationalist from top to bottom like me. It comprehends neither Turk nor Greek.

I went home exhausted that evening. The psychological pressure made me more tired than the tiredness one gets from work. Christiana as usual received me with a kiss, as every time I come home from work. After putting our daughter Nefeli to bed I told her about my experience and my feelings. She told me about her experience and feelings about the baby. As if her physiological tiredness was not enough, I was putting psychological pressure on her. Important things were happening in my life for the first time and Christiana was not going to be there for reasons outside her control. I was going to go through hundreds of experiences, but the important people in my life were not going to share my feelings.

The best thing I could do would be to relate all those feelings in the best possible way to my life's great friend, my wife. But I must not put her under any unnecessary burden. I thought I have to find a kind of balance.

PART -VI

INTERVIEWING THE WITNESSES

What difference does it make to the dead, the orphans and the homeless, whether the mad destruction is wrought under the name of totalitarianism or the holy name of liberty or democracy?

Mahatma Gandhi

The following day we went back to the area of the three villages. We knocked on doors hoping for an interview. After a lot of this, we reached Kazım Ereş's house. He was the first witness of the great crime to volunteer to speak. While preparing for the shoot we gleaned some information from him.

"There was a lot of military movement in the village twenty-four hours before the mass murder. A Greek I knew from Peristeronopigi asked me whether I was still alive while he was passing by in his car. I was suspicious that something was going to happening so I told the villagers to be careful. The following morning we heard gunshots, and we ran and hid. There were small foxholes around there, and we hid in those. Greeks coming from

Peristeronopigi started gathering the villagers. I saw from where I was hiding that they were taking women and children. One of them was calling my name to make me come out. But I didn't. The Greeks then took all of them outside the village and killed them."

Just when we were about to set the camera running his wife interrupted and started swearing. While she was shouting she was unconsciously giving her own statement, while Mustafa tried to calm her down.

"You've collected the Greeks and brought them here? What kind of a Muslim are you?"

"Auntie, these are Turks."

"They're not Turks as they say. I've heard they are Greek. I never talk to Greeks. I kick out the ones who come visiting. I throw stones at them as well... If you bring someone like that... You brought one Greek to Athlar yesterday so they say... will they come again to kill us?"

"Auntie..."

"For weeks we came home and even didn't find our bread to eat because they had chucked it away in the street."

"Auntie, do you know why this one is here? He's here to learn all these things that happened."

"Never! I'm telling you... I ask you.... If you bring Greeks to his area I don't take responsibility for the outcome. My eyes don't see too clearly, but your taxi has Greek number plates. They come here a lot. Greeks come here. But I found out my kids were... well... I pulled a knife on them!"

"You're right."

"Then another Greek came... him too... This is a Turkish village. Is it a Greek village? Are there any Greek houses? Our village is Turkish. We saved our own lives by hiding in caves. They looked for us as if hunting animals. Why was this man saved? Ask him where he was then. He survived by getting into a foxhole."

Even the diplomatic Mustafa could not calm her. We packed our things and left. If she stirred up the area important things could emerge I thought.

We went to the primary school where the children of the villages had once studied. I had goose bumps. I saw the photograph taken a couple of months before they were killed. I stood where I thought the photographer had stood imagining the children looking at the lens and smiling. There was a whole life ahead of them. Death was not something which would cross their minds. They only knew playing games, and listening to tale on their mother's warm lap. Mustafa's mobile interrupted my dreams and my flow of tears. It was Özmert. He had convinced his father to talk on camera.

We went to the family's poor-looking house where Özmert was waiting for us with some other relatives. I understood that the relatives were there to give him spiritual support. The pain I saw in Ali Faik's eyes was the greatest pain I have ever discerned in a human being. It was enough to make his eyes watery thinking that he had to talk about the scars he had tried to hide for so many years. From the moment I looked into his eyes it was clear that there was a vast scar in his heart, but he had covered it so very carefully, allowing no one near it.

I do not know how I managed to climb over his defenses and look into the depths of his sorrow, but it happened. I found myself sharing with him the  anger that poured out of him, the thoughts of the women and the children he had loved and that he had lost.

Everyone around me was talking in Turkish, but from the tone I figured out that Ali had changed his mind and would not speak to us. My only hopes were Mustafa's talent for communication and Özmert's efforts at emotional blackmail. If Ali had joined the ranks of those who would not be interviewed I would have lacked the material to make the film. In the end he was persuaded to tell his story.

He was taken as a captive to Limassol. When he came back he did not find anyone at home. His sixteen-day-old daughter Selden, two year-old Özlem, four-year-old Gulden and twenty-eight-year-old Mualla, his mother and all relatives were found in the mass graves.

I then listened to Beraat, the cousin of the village imam and teacher, Hasan Nihat, relate what she learned from her uncle about the apprehension of his family, and they were truly shocking details.

A Greek had taken Ali's wife and children from their home. This Greek was a friend of Ali's. Their fields were next to each other. They used to sit outside together on summer nights. They were like brothers. Ali's wife, holding her baby in her arms, asked the Greek to go home and get the baby's bottle. The Greek told her not to be upset and that they would give her another bottle at the place where they were going. They tied the other two children to their wrists so they could not run away. The little boy, younger than the others, was running to catch up with his mother. That was his last day. He got on the bus of death with the other villages and vanished forever.

Now, what happened to the murderers? They carried on with their lives as if nothing had happened. Nobody pursued them. No one called them to account for what they had done. Of course, I would not know if their consciences let them sleep at night. I also cannot know whether they came back from Australia in order to purge themselves of their sins. What have they got to be scared of? They did their duty to the state. They "killed the dogs".

In Atlılar thirty-seven women and children were killed and buried in the mass grave dug up behind the village. In Sandallar eighty-nine women, children and old people were murdered. The place they chose to murder them was a rubbish dump. After murdering them they burnt them and, using a bulldozer, they then mixed their dead bodies with the rubbish. During this process, the bodies were dismembered. The United Nations had to count the heads they collected in order to register the number of corpses.

The only Greek account I could find of these murders was written by Nicos Genias in Haravgi newspaper on 20 July 1998. Genias was passing by Sandallar and

Muratağa as the murderers were finishing off their business. He says:

"EOKA B people were digging pits with a bulldozer and putting the old people and babies from the village they had killed into them. One of them even boasted, "We did our duty..."

The subject of my thirty minute documentary, "the Voice of Blood" is this crime. It is this information that is barred from being shown on television. But I cannot keep quiet. I will not let go until everybody in the Greek community has found out what happened in these villages. A certain journalist has alleged that my entire aim is to make accusations. What I have, rather, is a massive sense of regret for things past, and a great desire to see a new start for our children.

I had to give a voice to Selden. She needed to call out to the hearts of both communities by means of imprisoning my conscience. How could I stop her? Selden is looking for her murderers. She is asking why they denied her the love of her father, and why they denied from him her love. Selden is saying one more thing: she is saying "put the weapons down. Do not let drums of war sound again; do not let the screams of death to be heard again. This island is too small to be drowned in blood." She is saying, "Our population is too small to hate each other so much."

I went home in the evening thoroughly shaken. The world inside me had changed forever. There was no space for hatred any more. Not even for my enemy. Hatred kills. I want no part of it ever again. And that night I cried as never before. It was as if all the sins of the state had come and made a little nest inside me. For the first time in my life I was scared of the power of hatred, and I understood the greatness of love. It was 19th August. It is impossible for me to forget this date because it was the date when I first received an e-mail from Özmert, and I am still keeping it in my inbox. It was the beginning of a great friendship.

Hi Tony
How are you?
My name is Özmert. I live in Aloa (Atlılar).
You came to us today and I'm sending you this e-mail so that you can have my e-mail address. Anyway, I want to talk about today. I don't know what you think about us but I've met a Greek who thinks like you for the first time. You told us that you were a human being as you were leaving our house. Yes, you're right. I believe you're a human being because you proved it as you were leaving today.
Don't get my dad wrong, these are sad memories for my dad.

In the morning Özmert wrote again:

I would like to talk about my dad's past.(Please don't cry Tony.) When my dad talks about his children he sometimes says: If Greeks hadn't killed my children in 1974, my elder daughter would be 37 years old. How can you ask me not to cry for our father's pain?

Özmert.

PART -VII-
WHO IS RESPONSIBLE?

"When a whole nation is roaring Patriotism at the top of its voice, I am fain to explore the cleanness of its hands and purity of its heart."
Ralph Waldo Emerson

Before I continue telling my story, I would like to give you some important information which is not in the documentary, either because it was given to me later, or I did not think it was important at the time.

What happened in Murataǧa, Sandallar and Atlılar is very important because it both shows the magnitude of the hatred against Turkish Cypriots in some quarters, and also how the murders managed to disappear.

The murderers of the women and children of the three villages are most certainly five to six members of EOKA B from Peristeronopigi. They have been identified by witnesses. The operation started in Murataǧa at around five o'clock in the morning. The murderers came with a bus which generally traveled from Peristeronopigi to Famagusta. At the entrance to the village they collected whoever they could find and put them all on the bus. Then they went away. The only person they murdered in the village itself was a shepherd. A short distance from where the shepherd was killed, the son of the village teacher was hiding, and therefore survived. He told me what happened.

According to the statement of Kazım Ereş and other Turkish Cypriots, Greek National Guardsmen were continuously patrolling these villages. There is no statement alleging they took part in any of the killings, but a thought does spring to mind. How could it be that such massacres could take place in three villages without the military noticing a thing? In statements given by people who are dead, witnesses claim to have heard a mainland Greek accent. If this is so it proves the presence of at least one mainland Greek person at the scene of the crime, most probably a junior officer.

I did not manage to find out which army units were in that area in August 1974, but it would be interesting to find out through the research of others. I was satisfied with what I had discovered.

According to what Beraat heard from her uncle and passed on to us, the soldiers patrolling the villages were raping the women over and over again. It is important to note that the men of those villages at that time were interned in Limassol. According to Andreas Dimitriou's statement of 21st November 2004 in the Alithia newspaper (Andreas is a well-known member of EOKA B), the soldiers in Tohni also engaged in rape. This question comes to mind: Was all this planned beforehand, or was it a sudden spasm of fanatical nationalism? What was interesting was that the same crimes as were committed in Famagusta were committed against men from Tohni in Limassol. Was this all a coincidence? Or was there an evil premeditated element to it?

While we were preparing the second version of the documentary, I asked some Greek Cypriot politicians to say on camera who gave the order to carry out the killings. They refused. Why would that be? If they have any courage, they must speak out. One can tell that they know something.

According to the Greek Junta's plans for the coup - "Ifestos " - comprising three parts, Aphrodite A, B and C, in the case of Turkey landing on the island all Turkish enclaves were to be eliminated. I have read some original orders pertaining to the Ifestos plan signed by Haralambos Hios and Giorgitsis. It was anticipated that the public would be psychologically prepared for the destruction of the Turkish Cypriots.

"Had Turkey not intervened, I would not only have proclaimed Enosis but I would have annihilated the Turks in Cyprus as well."

Nikos Sampson
(Eleftherotipia 26 February 1981)

Had Turkey not intervened, and had the Junta acquired control of the government, what kind of a future would have awaited the Turkish Cypriots? According to Sampson's statement above and the "Ifestos" plan, what happened in Murataǧa was just the overture.

For Turkish Cypriots, Sampson was the Omorfita murderer. The hatred he had for Turks was well known. Asking Turkish Cypriots to accept a Sampson ruling over them was rather like asking Jews to accept being ruled by Hitler.

Archbishop Makarios said these words on 19th July 1974 from the podium of the Security Council: *"As I have already stated the events in Cyprus do not constitute an internal affair of the Greek Cypriots. The Turkish Cypriots are also affected. The coup of the Greek junta is an invasion and from its consequences all the people of Cyprus, both Greek and Turks will suffer."*

However, after August 1974 the Junta ruled no more. Responsibility then reverted to the legal (or as some would say, semi-legal) government of the island. Therefore, responsibility, though widely evaded, had to sit with the Republic of Cyprus. If the guilty parties had been tracked down and brought to justice, this responsibility would have been discharged. But to date no one has been prosecuted for any offences against the Turkish Cypriots. And the Turkish Cypriots, in the light of this omission, see the Greek Cypriots as a whole as being to blame.

I have been accused of "leading a very suspect campaign of accusations against Greek Cypriots." So I should keep quiet and let this monstrous crime slumber beneath the carpet of history. So, in the end I am the criminal and traitor for bringing these matters to public attention. Me, that is, not the responsible individuals. They are absolved, whereas I must live as a traitor until I die. Cicero once said: "No one can save the one who closes his ears to the truth, and does not want to hear the truth from his friend."

The story of the mass executions becomes even more tragic as time goes on. This became the reason for many innocent Greek Cypriots, who had no connection to the crimes, to be executed. But the real criminals were able to escape without any punishment. Hasan Nihat, the teacher of Murataga village, before he died, related that he was advised to take his revenge on Greek Cypriot captives. He replied that he knew who the guilty parties were, and he would not avenge himself on the innocent. Alas, not everyone is as level-headed as Hasan Nihat. Consider that you come home to see your wife and children dismembered and tipped onto the rubbish dump, and that you are told that Turks had done the deed. You cannot convince me that such things would not turn a normal balanced man into a sick murderer. I would throw my pen away if the opposite happened. And of course, revenge killings also fall into the category of barbarism.

Here we can see the reason for a great deal of Greek Cypriots' incomprehension of my making this documentary. They have their hatred based on personal loss - all too valid reasons. The Turkish Cypriot of Murataǧa who lost his family feels the same.

I will not say that the Turks committed no crimes. If I were to say such a thing I would not be reading history straight. But I will say this. When Turkish generals observed acts of barbarism being carried out on Greeks in 1974, generally acts of revenge, they sent the prisoners concerned to Turkey for their safety. There were officers who killed their prisoners, and there were officers who saved them. I also want to say that I know stories of Greek Cypriots executing Turks as well as Greek Cypriots who were supporters of Makarios. I also know of Greek Cypriots who risked their lives to save Turks.

What am I trying to say here? There are no barbaric societies, only barbaric individuals. I know a great deal about Greek and Turkish brutality; I also know hundreds of kind and decent Greek and Turkish Cypriots.

What is the aim of this documentary and the others which will follow? It is to show my people (all Cypriots are my people) that war causes hatred, and war can only lead to disaster. In war there are no losers and there are no winners. In war there are only the dead, and women in black amid the ruins. This is why I say that hatred should cease. Otherwise one day we will face another Murataǧa or Assia incident.

It is not of the first importance if people hate me because of my work, provided they can be helped out of their wider hatreds by my efforts. I do not work for the present generation anyway, but for the one which will follow. I well know that with this documentary I am going against the demons of nationalism, the fearsome parts of nationalism which has been gnawing at our nations for years. But we must look the facts in the eyes and say "NEVER AGAIN."

"The weak can never forgive. Forgiveness is the attribute of the strong"
Mahatma Gandhi

It is easy to talk about the crimes of the Turks against the Greeks. Likewise it is easy to do the reverse. It is only when both sides have reached the necessary maturity, and have summoned the courage to apologize to each other that we can start the countdown to a solution. There is no shame in accepting one's mistakes; the shame is in concealing one's mistakes and letting the next generation quietly inherit horrors they had no part in.

It is actually impossible to forget about these crimes because in Cyprus there are monuments built over them to remind us. But consider how small an island we inhabit, and yet between 1963 and 1974 we see bodies secretly dumped on both sides. And we have managed on such a small island to lose track of our compatriots, the Turks, and they to lose track of us. The war drums must stop. Our children and grandchildren must not grace the next mass graves. I am not so much concerned with the type of solution that our politicians are trying to bargain into being, as much as with the hatred and suspicion, lodged in the brain for years.

PART -VIII-
WARNING FORM A CLOSE FRIEND

"The greatest respect that can be offered to truth is to follow it."

Ralph Waldo Emerson

Selden was the strongest voice I heard from the opposite shore of life. I left a short poem which I wrote for her at Atlılar the last time I visited the place. It was a small mark of respect to the youngest victim of this tragedy.

Selden,
I do not know if sixteen days was enough
for you to understand
that this world is not big enough
to encompass your innocence.
But believe me it is not.
It is a very cruel place Selden.
While the bullets were stamping your eyes shut,
all our lives stopped.
Selden,
your shadow is still here.
I saw your smile in the soul of a cloud.
Selden,
I wish a simple apology could be enough.

Özmert took the poem away from the cemetery in case someone saw the Greek writing on it and defaced it. It is now in his bedroom, like a symbol of the friendship between our families. My soul met Özmert's father's soul in the middle of a bridge of sorrow. Ali's tears mixed with mine in our mourning for his tragedy. Now I call him Father, and he greets me like a son.

And so, as I say, I find myself trapped in the Green Line. Who can keep me from my father's side in the North, or from my father's side in the South? I think I would die of sorrow if one day the checkpoints were to close again. Özmert sends me e-mails every night. He shares his life and his dreams with me. I love him with all my heart and will not let any checkpoint separate him from me.

Hi Tony!

Today we lived a very emotional afternoon. When I went to the martyrs and took your poem, firstly I looked its header. It was so impressive for me. Then I returned to the car and while I was driving, I read your poem. I called out to my mom immediately. She was inside the house. I read your poem to her, and she too was impressed. Then my brother came to the house and I called him into my room. I put the poem in his hand. Then when he finished reading, he looked into my eyes. I saw tears in his eyes. Finally at dinner, my sister showed it to my father and he read it. Also, he was impressed. Shortly everyone is impressed by your poem which I read today.

73

Hi Tony!

I always ask when I am alone, or before sleeping, when I put my head on the pillow; why Tony do that? Why he is searching this tragedy? I ask what the starting point of this research is. How he decide to start? I am thinking. But I didn't find any answer. Yes, you told me before. Righteousness is above nationality. But this is very risky for you and your family. Be carefully... I promise I will save this poetry all my lifetime. And I want to tell you a million times thank you, but I know this is not enough for you.

Thank you Tony, Bye!

Özmert and I have solved the Cyprus problem. The solution that the politicians have been looking for was right under our noses, but we could not see it. All that is necessary is to share pain, understanding; to cooperate, to support each other, to mix our sweat, our tears and our hearts. Only then can there be a political solution which will sort out the Cyprus problem from its very roots. The way to the solution of the problem goes through our hearts, not papers.

Hi Tony

How are you?
I took the CD from my friend. I gave him the film to convert into CD. I watched it with my brother and my sister's husband. We all cried together at end of the film. And in the evening we watched it all together with my father, mother and sister. They also found it good.

Firstly my father didn't want to watch it but then he watched. Anyway, I don't know if I will come to your baby's baptize party. If I say yes, then I must come there. If I give you a promise and then I can't come, I will be very upset. As I mentioned before, it depends on my work on the field... Take care my friend.

PART-IX-
TASHKENT / TOHNI

"It is error alone which needs the support of government. Truth can stand by itself."

Thomas Jefferson

We climbed up the foothills of Beşparmak Mountains at around ten in the morning. The Greek map in my hand said that the name of the village was Vuno. The Turkish map gave the name Tashkent to Tohni village. In 1974, the first group of people who were allowed to cross to the North after it had been established that their menfolk had been killed, were Turkish Cypriots of the Tohni village. Mustafa told me that the people in the north call this the village of widows.

There is a monument at the entrance of the village with pictures of the missing from the area. Of course, everyone knows the missing are in fact dead. And over the years no one has had the courage to return the bones, leaving that issue to long debate. Who will open the mass graves? Which one first? In the meantime, the mothers, whose hearts burn with pain, are denied a fit burial for their loved ones.

Suat Huseyin Kafadar was not at home, but the kids in the street pointed us in the direction of his farm. I could see his bald head as I remembered it from our previous meeting, bobbing amid the cows and the dung. He is

76

always kind, and he always smiles. One can't help thinking: How can someone who went through what he did simply get on with these daily jobs?

 We arranged it so that we would do the interview the next day in the morning. When we arrived again, Suat met us with his warm smile. Without wasting any time he told us how he had cheated the angel of death. Suat, who was then seventeen years old, is the only Turkish Cypriot who survived the mass murder. He told us how he returned from death to life.

"Armed Greek Cypriots came to our villages with policemen on 14th August 1974, and took all the men of the village away. They took us to the Greek Cypriot primary school and kept us there until evening. There were other Turkish Cypriots from Mari and Zigi with us there. We were over 100 people but then they sent the old and the children away, so our number went down to around 80. The next day buses came at around lunchtime. They put us on the buses. My dad, brother, uncle and cousins were with me.

We set off to Limasol accompanied by four men armed with automatic weapons. I didn't know them. They weren't from our village. Judging by their ages and appearance I could tell they weren't professional soldiers. There was a road block in Yermasoya area, so they stopped us. The policeman asked us who we were. One of the Greek Cypriot gunmen sarcastically said 'They are tourists'. From Limasol, we turned left and carried on towards Aya Fila. I knew that area because I had been working there. I remember that after passing the village towards Palodya there were sharp turns. We stopped by the side of the road. They put us in line and made us get off the bus one by one. We followed a truck on the left hand side of the road. There were two retaining walls 100 metres from the road. They gathered us there. One retaining wall was in front of us, the other behind. There were tents opposite us and they said that they were prison camps - but we didn't see any movement there. Three of the armed men were on top of the wall. One of them came down the wall in front of us. He told us to hand over our identity cards one by one. This took us ten minutes.

Suddenly the man at the bottom of the retaining wall shot one round. This was a signal. They started shooting like crazy. I was slightly injured in my side, and I fell to the ground. A friend of mine's corpse fell on top of me. I stayed where I was without moving. I was holding my breath. When the shooting stopped I heard the moaning. One of the armed men said "Hang on - they're not dead." They checked, I heard one or two shots, and the moaning stopped. They didn't know that I was alive because my friend's brain had split open on my head. They thought it was mine. They discussed for some time whether to take our watches or not. Then they decided not to in case the watches became evidence against them. They said they'd bring a bulldozer and left.

When I got up the scene was indescribable. There were two more people alive, but they were badly injured. One of them asked me to take him with me, but one of his legs was severed and it would have been impossible for me to carry him. The other one wanted me to escape as soon as possible and tell the world what had happened. A bit further off from where the murders took place there was a wooded area. I hid there until dark. When I saw that the sun had set and no one had come to bury the dead, I ran away. For four days I hid in the daytime and walked at night. In the end I managed to get to Mutluyaka. They helped me hide there. They contacted Dr. Ayten of Limasol Turkish Hospital, and I was taken to the Episkopi base with the help of the Red Cross. Then I was helped to cross to the north."

Once the interview had finished and the cameras were switched off, Suat said to me over coffee, "Do you know I voted yes in the referendum? Whatever happened, it happened thirty years ago. My father and brother are not coming back. We must have peace now, and not repeat the past. We are all Cypriots, and this is our land."

He lost his father and brother in such a way, and yet he suppresses his hatred and speaks in favor of peace. For this, he deserves a Noble peace prize. But then what would a farmer know about such prizes? He evaded bullets, exited the jaws of death and got on with his life.

After the interview Suat put on his hat and lost himself amid the hay and the cattle.

PART -X-
TIME TO APOLOGIZE

*"Patriotism is your conviction that this country is
superior to all other countries because you were
born in it."*

George Bernard Shaw

It was time to get Mustafa going. "Mustafa, it's time
you got a move on. We can't make a documentary with
what we've got so far. You've got to convince BRT to
give us archive materials and to let us use their
production facilities."

Mustafa is practical and active - provided he is
convinced of the importance of the task to hand. If your
argument isn't right, forget it. During our shoots we
became like brothers. Our hearts were set on the same
goal. He believed in what he was doing and did all he
could do to help. Perhaps at the fore was a curiosity as to
how long this crazy Greek was going to keep this up.
The production stage was taxing for him, but he was
patient and eventually satisfied with the result.

Getting us access to BRT's production facilities
necessitated Mustafa's two mobile phones almost
catching fire. "Efendim" to one, "efendim" to the other.
In the end he managed not only to book us in for the next
day, but also to take over the whole place. We changed
the system and drafted half of the personnel. The girls in
the archive department were coming and going with

going with cassettes I had chosen, and the images I thought appropriate, and I started work on the voiceover text. At one point the production room was crowded. Two women came with their hands full of cassettes, two technicians were busy adding video footage, one technician was busy adjusting one of the keyboards to Greek characters, and another technician was trying to adjust the voice arrangements. It was like Armageddon, but joyful. Where are you Mum? Your son just started the third world war at BRT.

We put Raziye into play too. Her only sin was that she spoke Greek. I liked her from the moment she said "Kalimera sas," meaning "good day to you." No one uses the formal plural "you" to me. Karl Jung once said: "The meeting of two personalities is like the contact of two chemical substances: if there is any reaction, both are transformed."

Raziye is from Luricina. She grew up without a father. One lunch-time her father said he would go and get an onion from their field and return in five minutes. His return took weeks as he was kidnapped on the way and taken to Larnaka police station. He returned with his toe nails pulled off. That was the time when cannibals lived in Cyprus. He died a couple of months after that.

Raziye stayed with us to the end of the process. She would do her program in the mornings, and then come and help us until late afternoon. We would be the first ones to go to the station in the morning, and the last ones to leave, just in time to avoid being kicked out. Birgul was in charge of production. She did not speak either English or Greek. And I could not speak Turkish. Also, we had very different ideas about how to do things. Conflict flared up, but with Raziye and Mustafa's calming influence we settled down to the job.

Some time over the last two days, an English speaking director, Mehmet, came by. We saved a lot of time we had previously lost due to lack of communication. I wonder why they taught us French rather than Turkish at school. At least the Turkish would have had some use.

Despite all the technical difficulties and the tragic nature of the subject we managed to iron things out in one week. We did not have any other option  as the station was readying itself for winter programs.

One scene from this time I will never forget. We were placing photographs of the victims with Birgul and Mustafa at the end of the program to the accompaniment of slow and solemn music. Grandfathers, grandmothers, mothers with their children, those of the mass graves, filled the room and passed among us like ghosts, thanking us for writing their story. We all stopped what we were doing, perhaps for ten minutes, perhaps for a hundred centuries, seized by a sense that they were dying right now, and that there was nothing we could do to save them. It was an emotional moment, and for the first time the tough Mustafa let his guard drop along with his tears. We were seeing our mothers, fathers, brothers, sisters and children in front of our eyes.

I thought that while the film was not made with the latest technical equipment, what the hell? - We were making history. After thirty years, a Greek Cypriot was filming the Turkish Cypriots' drama for the first time. For the first time the martyred Turkish Cypriots were remembered and honored as if by one of their own by a Greek Cypriot.

This was an act of apology. It is a personal apology to those who were murdered by my compatriots, who for thirty years tried to silence the voice of blood that echoed from the earth. Finally God caught up with Cain just when he thought he would get away with it.

Neither Turkish nor Greek Cypriots will find their debt of guilt fully redeemed. Too much blood has been shed on both sides. Now is not the time for politicians but the hour for a great apology. It is not the politicians or the army who have opened the barricades. It is the universe that is giving us a chance to bring the two communities closer so we may set our hearts right. What a shame on us if we waste this opportunity. Because, if we do waste it, our children will die like us, with the music of peace still locked inside their hearts.

CONCLUSION

As I crossed the barricade for the last time I felt lost. So many things had happened in ten days. My life had interlocked with those of so many, both alive and dead. From now I could not really decide which community I belonged to.

Since that time I have been trapped in the green line. My spirit enlarged, like the sky, to encompass the world. Hatred blew out like a candle; forgiveness and hope for tomorrow, the promise of a better start, took its place. Cyprus is the only country I have. It is the only country for Turkish and Greek Cypriots. Our fathers hated, killed and divided. Let us not permit our children to ruin their lives in the same spirit of hate. Let us be the generation that puts a final stop to the hatred. Only then will our children take up the kind of future which is rightfully theirs. If we do not act, there may be no tomorrow.

I now dream that one day we will all meet at the green line, and celebrate the peace stretching from the northern to the southern shores. The time has come for a general rehabilitation. We must have the courage to speak out on right and wrong. The Hellenes must learn to face their sins. They must be able to say, "the Turkish Cypriot victims of Tohni are buried here." And by the same token, the Turkish Cypriots must find themselves able to say, "These are the Greek Cypriots we pitched into the well at Ayas." Then no politician would be able to bring this evil to our society again.

Today Cyprus does not need politicians with rhetorical talents. What Cyprus needs is leaders who know how to get on their knees. Just like Willy Brandt, Chancellor of Germany who went to Poland in 1970 and knelt down before the Warsaw ghetto to beg forgiveness on behalf of the German people for the crimes of the Nazis. Willy Brandt heard the voice of blood.

Unfortunately our country is ruled by politicians who build their careers on nationalism. For them, apologizing is considered a sign of weakness, and kneeling a massive embarrassment. They would not remain in politics for twenty-four hours without enemies to oppose. For most of them, a solution to the Cyprus problem would mean the end of their political lives. Their whole political approach is based on repelling the barbarians.

*"Because the sky was dark and the barbarians didn't
come, some came from the border,
And said there were no barbarians any more.
And now, what will become of us without the
barbarians? Those people were a kind of solution."*
Constantinos Cavafis

When I look at the turbulent modern history of Cyprus, the only things I can see are horrific crimes, mass graves and missing people. Politicians with blood on their hands carry on doing as they please in the political arena, justifying the crimes committed during that dark period. They implicitly refuse to bow in front of any monument which represents crimes that they were responsible for; refuse to accept any responsibility for the dead, burnt and buried.

I cannot keep silent any more. This peculiar state of affairs must come to an end. The enemy is not on one side or the other. The enemy has come to nest among us all. If we do not cast them out, these vampires will return. This is the resolution behind "Voice of Blood." This is how I crossed the barricades one August morning and never came back. But I did not stay there either. If one day you happen to be at one of the barricades on the green line, just look to your left and right for a minute. You will see me there holding the injured sky of my small country.

"How can a solution come if everyone is trying to gain more and more? Nobody yet has said "What can I give for a solution, what can I sacrifice to achieve peace?"

Tony Angastiniotis
Ataturk Cultural Center, Nicosia
27 June, 2005

THE NEWSPAPERS

*"I have come to the conclusion that politics are
too serious a matter to be left to the politicians."*
Charles De Gaulle

CYPRUS MAIL

'Frozen out':
Greek Cypriot battles to have documentary on
1974 killings aired

By Simon Bahçeli
Nov. 4, 2004

CYPRIOT filmmaker and writer Antonis Angastiniotis
says the media has effectively banned a film he made
portraying the mass killing of Turkish Cypriots in the
villages of Aloa, Maratha and Sandalari in 1974.

"We claim European standards, European principles,
European laws, but the TV channels didn't even ask to
look at the film," Angastiniotis told the Cyprus Mail
yesterday.

"Not even the Cyprus News Agency, which monitors
all the news coming out of Turkey and the north,
mentioned that all the media, the Turkish-language
organs were reporting on my film," he added.

So far, Angastiniotis' film has only been shown in the Turkish Cypriot north. But he says his target audience is not Turkish Cypriots but Greek Cypriots.

"All Turkish Cypriots know what happened in these villages. It's the Greek Cypriots who don't."

Angastiniotis' 30-minute film, titled The Voice of Blood, gives a detailed account of how dozens of Turkish Cypriot women and children of the three villages were killed and thrown into mass graves by Greek Cypriots from neighbouring villages in the period between the two Turkish invasions in 1974. It includes extensive footage and interviews with survivors of the attacks.

The filmmaker believes that despite Cyprus' European and democratic credentials, it still has problems coming to terms with its past.

"Let's face it: truth is truth. As a state you have to be able to face your faults, your mistakes, your history," Angastiniotis says.

Worse still, he believes there is an unhealthy attitude in the country that prevents people from airing their views if they are out of line with government policy.

"There is terror. Some people even believe there is a list of who said 'yes' and who said 'no' in the referendum."

Angastiniotis is frustrated at the problems he has had getting his film aired.

"The media is being controlled. There is no other way of putting it," he said, adding Sigma had strong connections with the Presidential Palace, CyBC was a state channel, the Church influenced Mega and Antenna had likewise backed the 'no' campaign. (In fact I said Antenna belonged to an EOKA B member)

Angastiniotis describes his project as "something I had to do".

"If I didn't do this I couldn't sleep at night, and if they want to stop me making films on this subject, they will have to shoot me".

He adds, however, that he is not trying to paint the Turkish Cypriots as victim and the Greek Cypriots as perpetrators.

"I never said the Turks did not commit war crimes. They did. But I am responsible for the Greek side. I hope a Turkish Cypriot has the guts to do what I have done and make a film about Turkish atrocities," he explains.

The film is the culmination of several years of collecting data from archives and from chatting with locals in coffee shops. It was completed in August this year.

He says he was inspired to make it when he realised there was a gap in the knowledge of his generation about the recent history of the island - especially regarding the events of 1963 and 64, which he believes are brushed over by Greek Cypriot interpretations of history.

But the film focuses on three villages on the plain between Nicosia and Famagusta and what happened there when the men of the village were being held in prisoner-of-war camps in Limassol and the Turkish invasion was underway.

"The Greek Cypriots of the neighbouring villages, along with army personnel attacked the village. They shot the children, the mothers and the old people left in villages" "For me it became a nightmare because all these years I had been convinced that everything we had done was right."

Speaking on behalf of CyBC television, Andros Pavlides told the Cyprus Mail he would like to see the film to assess whether it was suitable for broadcast, but that he had had "too little time" to do so. A spokesman for Sigma also said he had not seen the film because of time constraints. All other channels denied knowledge of the film or the filmmaker, despite Angastiniotis' insistence that he written to them all telling them of it.

CYPRUS OBSERVER

The man who refuses to hate

Frontpage

Tony Angastiniotis is a man with very few friends. The Greek Cypriot filmmaker's two documentaries about Greek Cypriot killings in four Turkish Cypriot villages in the summer of 1974 have caused much heat in those parts of Cyprus where they were allowed to be shown. Cyprus Observer features an exclusive interview with Tony Angastiniotis, the man who has been dubbed as a 'notorious traitor' in the south of the island, and a 'lunatic' in the north. Coinciding with the interview, on Sunday, in the villages of Murataga, Sandallar, Atlılar, and on Monday in Taskent, commemoration of these events will take place.

Truth for the sake of Truth

*Tony Angastiniotis, 39-year-old Greek Cypriot filmmaker and journalist, talks openheartedly to **Arda Kuran** of <u>Cyprus Observer</u> about his recent documentaries, his upcoming book, the controversies around his work and his name, his life today and his dreams for tomorrow.*

ARDA KURAN - Two recent documentaries - Voice of Blood I and II - about atrocities committed against innocent Turkish Cypriots in the villages of Sandallar

91

(Sandalari), Murataga (Maratha), Atlılar (Aloa) and Taskent (Tochni) in the summer of 1974 have caused much heat in and Cyprus, in fact, in those parts of the island where they were allowed to be shown. The storm is mainly generated by the fact that the mind and the muscle behind them is a Greek Cypriot. Surprisingly however, it looks as if Tony Angastiniotis, inescapably christened "one of the nastiest traitors and Turk-lovers ever" in the south of the island, doesn't have too many friends in the North either. Many people are cynical towards a Greek Cypriot so deeply and vigorously concerned with such a subject.

Awfully dubious myself as to whether this man was a complete nutcase or I was just too shallow to grasp his out-of-this-world compassion for humanity and peace, I sped off to Famagusta to meet the man and find out for myself.

Angastiniotis' Voice of Blood I and II are similar in the sense that they are both the same story; the massacres executed by EOKA B around the time of the Turkish intervention in the summer of 1974. According to their director, the first film was "not up to the desired standard", not only because he did not have the necessary equipment and technology at his service but also because the villagers he wanted to interview were "suspicious as to what a Greek Cypriot was trying". So with great help from Famagusta's Eastern Mediterranean University (EMU) in terms of equipment and permission to use their facilities, Tony took his time and "managed to produce Voice of Blood II which he considers better and closer to his original dream.

TESTIMONY

Voice of Blood II depicts several villagers who 'survived' the massacres, lost their entire families and in some cases, their entire village folk. Some of the interviewees, Ali Faik for example, returned to his village from Limassol after 110 days at a prisoners of war camp, only to find his house deserted and his wife and three children, including 16-day-old Selden, slain.

"The Sandallar story is one of the most dramatic events of 1974, or in fact of the whole conflict between two nationalities," Tony says.

He truly believes in what he is doing. But what is he doing, really? Questions concerning this man's exact intentions were firmly fixed in my mind during our meeting and I needed answers.

"People think my films are propaganda, but when they watch them, when they see that I don't twist stories or water them down, they know they can trust me," Angastiniotis says. "The villagers used to refuse to give interviews to me in the past because they didn't want to be used for propaganda. After they watched the first film, they started believing. They realised I was doing this for the information itself, that I was trying to get the real story out. It's time for the world to know the reality in Cyprus, and time for Cypriots to know the reality themselves."

"Around the time of the referenda, nationalism was very fiery in the South," the director continues. "There was fighting in the streets and car windows were broken because they had 'Yes' stickers on them. I used to wear a 'Yes' badge on me every day, and I felt the strong wave of hostility towards me. I realised that the Greek Cypriots are living in total ignorance. Ignorance has allowed Greek Cypriot propaganda about the 'barbarian Turks' to work on their minds."

Angastiniotis clearly states that he did not try to justify the events of 1974 by making these documentaries. His truth is beyond who is right and who is wrong, he says. That doesn't sound that irrational.

"The Turkish army came with weapons, airplanes and arms," he says. "Whether you want to call it 'peace operation' or 'invasion', the title is not important. The thing is that it was a war. When we use weapons between two peoples, we call it war. During that war both sides committed sins. Yet, the average Greek Cypriot has no idea about atrocities committed against Turkish Cypriots. For this reason they have a nationalistic spirit that hinders them to understand the pain of the other community. They think they are the only ones who suffered, that only they are refugees, that only they have missing people. An average Greek Cypriot doesn't know there are missing Turkish Cypriots. He is shocked to hear that.ᕐ My target was always to show to the Greek nationalist spirit that we are no less barbaric than any other. And that we have also committed atrocities. Of course, not everybody. When we accuse a whole nation of barbarism, then 'a good Turk is a dead Turk'. If you emphasise this, then I cannot be your brother."

94

Angastiniotis eagerly awaits the day the Greek Cypriots will accept that they have also committed bad deeds and that they are responsible for having created certain circumstances which led to the Turkish intervention of 1974. He does not stop at accepting the wrongdoings, but he goes on to say that Greek Cypriots need to apologise for what they have done to their fellow islanders to this day, and vice versa. He wants Papadopoulos to go to the martyrs' cemetery of Sandallar and apologise on his and his community's behalf for the killings. "Only then will we be able to move away from the ethnocentric idea that the 'other' is an inferior creature," he says. "I am trying to hit out at our nationalisms-that's my goal - to target our thinking that 'we did nothing wrong'. I know if that myth collapses then we have a better foundation to build a friendship."

But as his documentaries are not even considered for screening on Greek Cypriot TV channels and cinemas, how can Angastiniotis achieve his goal? He has a very interesting and confident answer.

"If they don't want to show it in the South now, I will take my films to different festivals around the world. It will leave Cyprus from Ercan Airport, will go around Europe and return to Larnaca. If this film is shown at an international film festival, whether it wins or not, Greek Cypriots will hear about it and will start ask questions. They will want to know why it was not shown in the country of its origin. I want to generate that kind of pressure so that the TV stations will at least be forced to see it. Then they can interview me if they want."

One famous traitor-bashing against Tony took place on Sigma Radio last year, when people who had not even watched the documentaries, to put it nicely, 'commented' on the man and what he does. Tony says he does not mind being invited to a programme during which Greek Cypriots will call him a 'traitor' or a lot worse as it usually happens, as long as he can argue against it. More often than not though, he is not there to defend himself.

"If any clever journalist would invite me to his/her show and attack me with a strong hand, I'd gladly accept," he says. "This is what I would do if I was in their place."

PROPAGANDA

"Şener Levent accused me once of working with the nationalists on the Turkish side and becoming part of Turkish propaganda," Angastiniotis continues. "My answer to him and to everybody is this: On this island, there are nationalists, there are leftists, there are rightists, there is everything here. The problem in this island is that the right and the left don't speak to each other, neither one side to the other, neither in between the peoples. They are always trying to convert the converts. All the leftists sit together and talk with the leftists. Same with the rightists. But we are never going to make something of this island unless a leftist talks to a nationalist. They are part of the same society. They will have to find a way to get along. The old way is "kill them, get rid of them". But now it's 2005, and there is another way. We call it dialogue.

"As for Tony, Tony is not leftist, he is not rightist, Tony is an internationalist, something which the leftists wrongly adopted. I care for the interests of the whole world. The more you kill, the more fanaticism you create. I love the left, I love the right, I love communism, I love the nationalism. I love this island. I cannot hate you because you don't believe in the same things I believe in. I cannot hate you because you are Greek. I cannot hate you because you are Turkish. I refuse to hate. Because hatred destroys us."

Tony was not always so peaceloving, however. Once a fanatic EOKA B supporter, he grew up admiring Grivas and the like. At eight, he found a poster of 'Dighenis' lying in the street in his native Famagusta, picked it up and put it up on the door of their house. He says he is still unsure as to why, but it was just an innate respect and love for EOKA B that he had. The nationalistic environment in which he grew up, listening to stories of glorious battles against the British and the Turkish where the Greeks never surrender, led Tony to become a communist-hating Greek fanatic. He walked around Nicosia in a green beret with 'EOKA B' written in blue on it. He says he worshipped the Greek flag, which consequently means he was not so keen about the Turkish flag.

"If you love the blue flag, you must hate the red flag," Angastiniotis says. "It's part of nationalism, and this is what they feed you for 12 years of schooling every single day in the South."

I am ambiguous as to why exactly Tony turned around in the year 2002 all of a sudden, "out of sheer curiousity," as he says, to do research in order to find out what really happened on this island.

"When I found out that we killed children in Sandallar, that we were baby killers, I couldn't find any basis for my nationalism anymore," he explains. "We are also barbarians. We planned to destroy the 1960 Constitution and we produced the Akritas Plan. How could Samson be my favourite hero anymore?

But although I agree 100 per cent with what he says, I can't get myself to grasp the very idea of his immediate U-turn. Something else, something big must have triggered this, I think to myself. "When I had a proof that Samson executed, with his own hands, innocent people in Kaimakli, I opened the dustbin, threw my nationalism inside, and closed that bin," says Tony.

Yet again, I don't know of any other Greek Cypriot who would take such drastic measures to show their abhorrence vis-à-vis Hellenic nationalism. Not in Cyprus. Is there any other Greek Cypriot who tries to open the dustbin for others so that they also can dump their "ignorant nationalism" into there? Tony seems like a lone legionnaire to me, but is this enough to judge the man 'insincere'?

What else can I ask a man who tells me he loves both Greeks and Turks of Cyprus so much that he refuses to go to the military and to be only on one side of the line? What more can I tell a man who gets death threats regularly, and laughs as he tells me about them?

What would you do if there was a war in Cyprus today," I ask. "I would stand on the Green Line and get shot from both sides," is Angastiniotis' answer.

(Tony says he has waited for enough time for Papadopoulos to implement his Plan B, which he had deemed better than the Annan Plan. Now he is planning on moving to Famagusta with his family and newly born baby, where he will be teaching at the EMU's School of Communications. While he is planning his work on a new documentary about the referenda of 2004, his book, Trapped in the Green Line, along with a VCD of his documentaries, is coming out on August 15 from Rustem Bookshop.)

The names and ages of the murdered people of Muratağa, Sandallar and Atlılar are as follows.

Name (Age)

Tülay Süleyman (27)
Hasan Süleyman (9)
Kemal Süleyman (6)
Okkan Süleyman (3)
Ayşe Hasan (55)
Narin Hasan (15)
Kıymet Hasan (20)
Gürhan Ali Çerkez (12)
Betül Hüseyin (12)
Mualla Ali Faik (28)
Gülden Ali Faik (4)
Özlem Ali Faik (2)
Selden Ali Faik (16 günlük)
Fatma Tahir (40)
Emine Tahir (18)
Emine Hasan Muhammet (29)
Ahmet Hasan Muhammet (3)
Bahire Hasan Muhammet (3)
Hasan Kara Hüseyin (68)
Emine Rüstem (38)
Sezin Rüstem (15)
Mustafa Rüstem (13)
Erbay Rüstem (12)

Name (Age)

Şifa Hasan Kara Hüseyin (60)
Nadir Hasan Kara Hüseyin(24)
Meral Hasan Kara Hüseyin (20)
Fatma Kamil Meriç (26)
Vedia Kamil Meriç (6)
Yonca Kamil Meriç (4)
Ozan Kamil Meriç (3)
Hakan Kamil Meriç (2)
Kağan Kamil Meriç (12)
Fatma Mehmet Naci (50)
Şükran Mehmet Naci (22)
Soncan Mehmet Naci (14)
Erünsal Mehmet Naci (10)
Nazım Hüseyin (6)
Şadiye Şadan (48)
Ülkü Şadan (22)
Fatma Şadan (19)
Rahme Cemal (65)
Ayşe Bayram (8)
Mustafa Bayram (6)
Şerife Bayram (1)
Mehmet Osman (82)

100

Sibel Rüstem (10)
Raziye Hasan (75)
Mustafa Hasan (48)
Havva Mustafa (40)
Türker Mustafa (16)
Tacay Mustafa (13)
Zalihe Hüseyin (70)
Ayşe Süleyman (47)
Dinavaz Süleyman (16)
Zalihe Süleyman (15)
Emine Süleyman (14)
Aliye Süleyman (12)
Havva Süleyman (11)
Gültekin Süleyman (9)
Rasime Osman (45)
Sezay Osman (16)
Hüseyin Osman (95)
Ayşe Hüseyin Osman (88)
Emine Bayram (38)
Halil Bayram (11)
Eren Bayram (9)
Şifa Mehmet (60)
Ülfet Mehmet Salih (70)
Halil Hüseyin (65)
Emine Halil (60)
Cemaliye Hasan (42)
Rahmi Hasan (19)
Ayşe Hasan (15)
Ersoy Hasan (12)
Sevgi Hasan (10)
Uğur Hasan (9)
Özcan Hasan (6)
Erdoğan Aziz (45)

Zühre Mehmet (80)
Nadire Süleyman (70)
Enver Hüseyin (65)
Hasan Sadık (84)
Sevim Arif (15)
Seval Arif (12)
Hüseyin Arif (11)
Yüksel Arif (10)
Göksel Arif (8)
Şeniz Arif (5)
Hayriye Arif (4)
Derviş Sadık (70)
Havva Derviş (60)
Hatice Derviş (22)
Fatma Mehmet Tavukçu (35)
Mustafa Mehmet Tavukçu (10)
Talat Mehmet Tavukçu (8)
Mustafa Mehmet (55)
Ayşe Mustafa (50)
Okay Mustafa (14)
Dudu Ali Osman (70)
Mehmet Hüseyin (17)
Ertan Hüseyin (14)
Erdinç Hüseyin (12)
Naziyet Mehmet (50)
Rahmi Hasan (72)
Emine Mehmet Salih (80)
Güldane Mehmet (44)
Serpil Mehmet (19)
Sevgül Mehmet (18)
Mustafa Mehmet (17)
Semra Mehmet (14)
Hasan Mehmet (13)

Fatma Erdoğan (38)
Kadriye Erdoğan (11)
Zehra Erdoğan (9)
Ahmet Erdoğan (8)
Ayşe Erdoğan (3)
Emine Hüseyin (40)
Seval Hüseyin (19)

Savaş Mehmet (11)
Cengiz Mehmet (10)
Songül Mehmet (6)
Hasan Hüseyin Ali Çavuş (76)
Aziz Fikri (11)
Hüseyin Erdoğan (6)